Indicators For Oral Languag

Teachers can identify a child's phase of development by obser
It should be noted however, that most childre

Phases

Phase 5: Consolidated Language For Learning

Language and Literacy Behaviours

Language of Social Interaction

◆ **communicates effectively by sharing ideas, offering advice, opinion and information and reacting to contributions of others**

- shows an increasing awareness of social conventions, e.g. *Could you tell me where...? Mrs Carroll asked if you would...*
- reacts according to own perceptions in a conflict situation, but is able to appreciate another's point of view through adult mediation
- adapts language to meet different social and situational needs, talking to friends at netball is different from meeting friends of parents
- monitors others' speech and paraphrases content, e.g. *I felt really angry when the group wouldn't co-operate*
- uses intonation, facial expressions and gestures as tools for communicating ideas and feelings
- uses jargon or slang with peers

Language and Literacy

◆ **recognises that language is adapted to meet social, situational and educational needs, e.g. the language of reporting is different from that of interviewing or story-telling**

◆ **demonstrates the ability to develop a topic in curriculum-related situations, e.g. reporting, describing, comparing**

◆ **interprets texts from own point of view — expresses opinions, draws conclusions**

◆ **uses appropriately specialised vocabulary and structures in a variety of situations, e.g. discussions, reports, debates**

- shows evidence of planning during recounts
- adds appropriate elaboration and detail to recounts and describes events, objects and concepts outside immediate experience, e.g. community news
- adds evaluative comments to enhance spoken presentations, e.g. *I believe that recycling is important and we all need to take it more seriously*
- demonstrates knowledge of difference between narrative and informational texts
- incorporates literary expressions when describing or discussing narrative texts, e.g. repetition of the phrase made the story flow
- is able to describe the setting, events and characters of stories/films/television dramas succinctly
- retells stories of some complexity, individually or in groups
- makes comparisons between narrative and informational texts
- uses similes and metaphors to enhance meaning
- shows knowledge of language structure, e.g. uses conjunctions effectively to express relationships between ideas; maintains and manipulates tones and mood appropriately; provides referents when using pronouns
- discusses rules of language, grammar
- recognises subtle differences in words, e.g. shimmery/shiny, cross/angry
- is able to describe the significant content of stories, television dramas and films succinctly

Language and Thinking

◆ **continues to develop reason and logic, by attempting to draw conclusions, make inferences, justify and explain statements; asking questions and seeking confirmation**

◆ **listens to evaluate, draw inferences and make judgements**

- investigates problems and sees a range of solutions
- offers definitions of words, usually by functions
- considers possible cause/effect relationships and justifies the most appropriate, e.g. *At first I thought it was the slope that increased the car speed but it could also be the smooth surface of the track*
- follows complex sequences of instructions
- evaluates the consistency of information across several sentences
- initiates questions to gain clarification or further information
- uses language for puns, jokes, riddles and sarcasm.

Phase 6: Extended Language For Learning

Language and Literacy Behaviours

Language of Social Interaction

◆ **selects and sustains language and style appropriate to purpose, context and audience e.g. formal, informal talk**

◆ **effectively interprets whether a message has been understood**

- takes into account another's point of view, e.g. *from your point of view this might be expensiv___ ___ ___ ___ ___portance.*
- needs and uses l___
- uses appropriate___
- is aware of audie___ ___ ___ ___ e history of mining in this ar___ ___ ___ ___ I will not go into too muc___
- refines use of ap___ ___ ___ ___ ___unicate ideas, feelings and information

Language and Literacy

◆ **summarises main ideas from written or spoken texts using succinct language**

◆ **draws conclusions from, makes inferences based on and evaluates written and oral text and is able to listen and respond to an alternative perspective**

◆ **describes events, objects and concepts outside immediate experience, e.g. world news**

- shows advanced planning of content when presenting information, e.g. in reports, summaries
- selects vocabulary for impact, e.g. to persuade, surprise
- uses language to reflect on and discuss written or spoken texts
- confidently and competently recounts events, providing detail and elaboration
- demonstrates fluency and a personal style when reading orally
- discusses rules of language, grammar

Language and Thinking

◆ **uses language to express independent, critical thinking**

◆ **uses oral language to formulate hypotheses, criticise, evaluate, plan and to influence the thinking of others**

◆ **deals with abstract ideas using concrete examples**

- listens to the ideas and viewpoints of others, using oral language to respond, expressing and modifying own opinions
- presents a variety of arguments to support a claim
- compares and contrasts observations, ideas, hypotheses with others
- explains understandings of topics, concepts, etc. providing convincing argument and evidence to support point of view
- recognises potential and limitations of words to persuade, explain, clarify, solve problems etc.
- answers spontaneous questions in an informed, competent manner, making sure that listeners understand what is being said
- uses language to paint 'word pictures'

Year: _____ Teacher: _____ Year: _____ T

Year: _____ Teacher: _____ Year: _____ T

e Developmental Continuum

ing that the child is exhibiting all the key indicators of a phase.
n will also display indicators from other phases.

Student's Name _____

I. D. _____

School _____

Phase 7: Proficient Language Use

Language and Literacy Behaviours

Language of Social Interaction

◆ **uses language to include or exclude others, e.g. paraphrasing technical terms to include audience**

- responds sensitively in a range of different contexts to the demands of audience and purpose, e.g. when making a visitor from a different socio-cultural background welcome at a barbecue.
- in conflict situation acknowledges different points of view.
- uses language to help reduce conflict
- uses language effectively to support, share understandings and experiences with and to influence others
- recognises potential social 'conflict' and is able to use language effectively to defuse the situation, e.g. being aware of and tactfully retrieving a social blunder, diverting attention from a divisive area or highlighting common ground between potential adversaries.
- paraphrases to clarify meaning.
- uses paraphrasing and restating to confirm understanding as listener
- uses language effectively to negotiate issues

Language and Literacy

◆ **uses language critically to reflect on and analyse spoken and written texts**

◆ **uses text structures and language features confidently according to purpose, context and audience, in cooperation with peers**

◆ **uses strategies such as note-taking to summarise spoken texts or to prepare for an oral presentation.**

- can compare and contrast different points of view
- is aware of the acceptable genre to suit context, audience and purpose and purposefully uses a deemed unacceptable genre to make an impact
- confidently and accurately uses subject-specific vocabulary
- uses quotations, similes and metaphors to enhance communication
- uses language effectively to achieve an effect, e.g. to conjure up a menacing atmosphere or to convey calmness and peace
- detects and challenges the use of words and phrases that impute stereotypes such as gender, age, race; and identifies language which conveys social values
- purposefully uses unbiased language

Language and Thinking

◆ **Uses language to reflect on learning and to further develop understanding, for example, can access own reaction to particular ideologies and positions, or recognises when further information is required to clarify understandings**

- uses language to construct effective arguments in relation to contentious issues
- manipulates use of language through sarcasm, jokes and subtle humour
- recognises the power of the spoken word to influence human behaviour
- is able to consider and reflect on two sides of an argument, make a judgement and find own position

Phase 8: Advanced Language Use

Language and Literacy Behaviours

Language of Social Interaction

◆ **shows sophisticated understanding of the power and effect of spoken language when speaking and listening.**

- negotiates agreements in groups where there are disagreements or conflicting personalities, managing the discussions sensitively and intelligently and concluding them with positive summaries of achievement
- uses talk to explore complex concepts and ideas to clarify her/his own and others' understanding
- asserts sustained points of view or ideas to both familiar and unfamiliar audiences with determination and conviction but without aggression, condescension or disrespect
- critically examines own reactions to spoken texts; is alert to own vulnerability to emotional and other seductive appeals and can dispassionately analyse the personal and linguistic reasons for this
- uses non-sexist and non-racist language
- anticipates likely disagreements between self and listeners, and structures material to minimise or overcome this by acknowledgement, for example: *I feel you may disagree with me about this but would you mind waiting until I've finished before you put your point of view*

Language and Literacy

◆ **interacts responsively, critically and confidently with both familiar and unfamiliar audiences on specialised topics in formal situations, and consistently achieves a variety of purposes in speech.**

◆ **analyses the characteristics of intended audiences and demonstrates psychological and interpretative insights in choosing approaches that suit audiences; chooses language calculated to appeal emotionally to specific audiences**

- identifies, challenges and justifies interpretations of the underlying assumptions, points of view and subtexts in spoken texts; identifies when what is said seems contrary to what the text itself suggests and justifies that interpretation with evidence from the text
- responds quickly and appropriately to people and situations to maintain an overall purpose; confidently and good-humouredly handles diversions and unexpected questions
- modifies content and approach when speaking to an unresponsive audience
- understands that people respond to both non-verbal and verbal elements of spoken language and works on enhancing interpersonal skills to improve communication with others

Language and Thinking

◆ **analyses spoken texts in terms of the socio-cultural values, attitudes and assumptions they convey**

◆ **responds to and analyses spoken texts outside own socio-cultural experience to enhance own knowledge and understanding**

◆ **identifies and analyses characteristics of a speaker's tone and style of presentation; what makes it bombastic, humorous, reasonable**

- examines texts for subtexts, significant inclusions or exclusions, for example, how males and females are presented, included or excluded
- discusses the power of language to reinforce or change values and attitudes
- infers meaning by using socio-cultural understanding of the purposes of particular text types and the motivations of individuals, such as public figures
- knows that vested interests may colour some individuals' views and listens carefully for clues to the subtext
- knows that the impartial appearance of text may be bogus and listens critically for bias, e.g. current affairs program items
- explores how analogies, imagery and other linguistic features affect the tone and mood of spoken texts and provide insight into the speaker's motives and opinions

ORAL LANGUAGE DEVELOPMENTAL CONTINUUM

The Oral Language Developmental Continuum was researched, developed and written by Jenny Evans, Education Department of Western Australia.

The framework outlined in the Continuum and Resource Book was developed by Leanne Allen, Speech Pathologist Consultant for the Education and Health Departments of Western Australia.

First Steps was developed by the Education Department of Western Australia under the direction of Alison Dewsbury.

STEPS Professional Development & Consulting
Salem, MA

STEPS Professional Development & Consulting
97 Boston Street
Salem, MA 01970
A division of Edith Cowan University Resources for Learning
Offices throughout the world

First published 1994 by Addison Wesley Longman
Previously published 1996 by Heinemann, USA
Currently published 2004 *STEPS* Professional Development & Consulting
on behalf of the Education Department of Western Australia

Library of Congress Cataloging-in-Publication Data
CIP is on file with the Library of Congress

ISBN 0-9746654-6-0
First Steps Oral Language Developmental Continuum

Contents

Part I: Foundations of First Steps   1

Linking Assessment to Teaching   2
Effective Learning: 'Pewit'   6
Effective Learning: 'The Three Rs'   10

Part II: About Oral Language   13

Effective Communication Diagram   14
The Oral Language Developmental Continuum   15
How To Use the Oral Language Developmental
Continuum   16
Oral Language Assessment for Children Where
'Language of Home' Differs from
That of the Teacher   18

**Part III: Phases of Oral Language
Development**   21

Phase 1: Beginning Language   22

Beginning Language Indicators   23
For Parents   24

Phase 2: Early Language   25

Early Language Indicators   26
Teaching Notes   27
Establishing an Environment for
Speaking and Listening   29
Speech Development   31
Language of Social Interaction   32
Language and Literacy   33
Language and Thinking   34
For Parents   36

Phase 3: Exploratory Language   37

Exploratory Language Indicators   38
Teaching Notes   39
Establishing an Environment for
Speaking and Listening   41
Speech Development   43
Language of Social Interaction   44
Language and Literacy   46
Language and Thinking   47
For Parents   49

**Phase 4: Emergent Language for
Learning**   50

Emergent Language for Learning
Indicators   51
Teaching Notes   52
Establishing an Environment for
Speaking and Listening   54
Speech Development   56
Language of Social Interaction   57
Language and Literacy   59
Language and Thinking   62
For Parents   64

**Phase 5: Consolidated Language for
Learning**   65

Consolidated Language for Learning
Indicators   66
Teaching Notes   67
Establishing an Environment for
Speaking and Listening   69
Language of Social Interaction   70
Language and Literacy   72
Language and Thinking   75
For Parents   77

**Phase 6: Extended Language for
Learning**   78

Extended Language for Learning
Indicators   79
Teaching Notes   80
Establishing an Environment for Speaking
and Listening   82
Language of Social Interaction   83
Language and Literacy   86
Language and Thinking   89
For Parents   91

Phase 7: Proficient Language Use   92

Proficient Language Use Indicators   93
Teaching Notes   94
Language of Social Interaction   95
Language and Literacy   97
Language and Thinking   99

Phase 8: Advanced Language Use   101

Advanced Language Use Indicators   101

Part IV: Profiles of Oral Language Development

Part IV: Profiles of Oral Language Development — 103

Student's Profile Sheets — 104
Whole Class Profile Sheets — 110
Whole Class Profile Sheets Key Indicators Only — 130

Acknowledgements — 136
Bibliography — 138

Part I

Foundations of First Steps

In this section the philosophical and theoretical framework of First Steps is set out. Specific points are made about the teaching of children for whom English is a second language and some suggestions are made about factors which foster effective learning in the classroom.

Foundations of First Steps includes:

- Linking Assessment to Teaching
    The Developmental Continua
    Teaching Strategies
    Underlying Theoretical Assumptions
    Important Considerations
    Teaching Children for whom English is a Second Language
- Effective Learning
    Problem Solving
    Embeddedness
    Working Memory
    Interaction
    Time
- 'The Three Rs'
    Reflecting
    Representing
    Reporting

Linking Assessment to Teaching

In an increasingly complex world, re-evaluating methods of teaching and learning is important. At the same time, methods of evaluating development, especially in relation to testing, have become highly problematic. Effective teachers have always used systematic observation and recording as a means of assessment. The First Steps materials have been developed to give teachers an explicit way of mapping children's progress through observation. The Developmental Continua validate what teachers know about children.

The Developmental Continua

The continua have been developed to provide teachers with a way of looking at what children can actually do and how they can do it, in order to inform planning for further development. It is recognised that language learning is holistic and develops in relation to the context in which it is used. However, given the complexity of each mode of language, a continuum has been provided for reading, writing, spelling and oral language, in order to provide teachers with in-depth information in each one of these areas.

The Continua make explicit some of the indicators, or descriptors of behaviour, that will help teachers identify how children are constructing and communicating meaning through language. The indicators were extracted from research into the development of literacy in English-speaking children. It was found that indicators tend to cluster together, i.e. if children exhibit one behaviour they tend to exhibit several other related behaviours. Each cluster of indicators was arbitrarily called a 'phase'. This clustering of indicators into phases allows teachers to map overall progress while demonstrating that children's

language does not develop in a linear sequence. The concept of a phase was shown to be valid by the Australian Council for Educational Research in their initial research into the validity of the *Writing: Developmental Continuum*.

Individual children may exhibit a range of indicators from various phases at any one time. 'Key' indicators are used to place children within a specific phase, so that links can be made to appropriate learning experiences. Key indicators describe behaviours that are typical of a phase. Developmental records show that children seldom progress in a neat and well-sequenced manner; instead they may remain in one phase for some length of time and move rapidly through other phases. Each child is a unique individual with different life experiences so that no two developmental pathways are the same.

The indicators are not designed to provide evaluative criteria through which every child is expected to progress in sequential order. They reflect a developmental view of teaching and learning and are clearly related to the contexts in which development is taking place. That is, language development is not seen as a 'naturalistic' or universal phenomena through which all children progress in the same way. Children's achievements, however, provide evidence of an overall pattern of development which accommodates a wide range of individual difference.

Teaching Strategies

The other major purpose of these documents is to link phases of development to teaching strategies, in order to help teachers make decisions about appropriate practice in the light of children's development. It is important that within this framework teachers value individual difference and cultural diversity. **It is not intended that these** strategies are prescriptive; they offer a range of practices from which teachers might select, depending upon the purposes of any particular language program and the needs of the children in their class. The purpose of the Continua is to link assessment with teaching and learning in a way that will support children and provide practical assistance for teachers.

Underlying Theoretical Assumptions

The First Steps indicators and suggested activities have been based on the following theoretical assumptions:

- Language learning takes place through interactions in meaningful events, rather than through isolated language activities
- Language learning is seen as holistic; that is, each mode of language supports and enhances overall language development
- Language develops in relation to the context in which it is used; that is, it develops according to the situation, the topic under discussion, and the relationship between the participants
- Language develops through the active engagement of the learners
- Language develops through interaction and the joint construction of meaning in a range of contexts
- Language learning can be enhanced by learners monitoring their own progress
- The way in which children begin to make sense of the world is constructed through the language they use and reflects cultural understandings and values

It is important that the indicators and activities are interpreted from the perspective of these underlying assumptions about language learning.

Important Considerations

The First Steps materials have been designed to help teachers map children's progress and suggest strategies for further development. When making decisions about what to do next, there are a number of issues that need to be considered.

Teachers' actions, strategies and ways of interacting with children reflect particular values and assumptions about learning. Through these interactions, children construct a view of what 'counts' as literacy in a particular classroom setting. This is manifested in the way:

a) teachers make decisions about selecting materials and texts
b) activities are carried out using the materials and texts
c) teachers talk with children
d) children talk with each other
e) what gets talked about (topic)

The decisions made by teachers play a role in how children come to understand what counts as literacy. In some cases there may be major conflicting and competing value systems at work leading to a variety of outcomes.

For example, the text Cinderella implicitly constructs a particular view of the world which presents women in a stereotypical role, not necessarily reflecting the role of women in modern society.

Clearly the text can be used in a number of different ways. It might be used as a shared book experience in which the teacher engages the children in a reading of the text, developing talk around the concepts of print and the repeated patterns of the text. In focusing on these aspects, the teacher would be constructing a view of reading which places emphasis on print rather than the message and leaves the role of women, as presented in the text, unchallenged. However, if the teacher encouraged the children to talk about the text in a way that challenged this view, through talking about their own experience of women and presenting other literature, the teacher would begin the process of helping children to detect the values within text.

Moving from this activity to asking the children to draw a picture of their own siblings and write a description about them, the teacher's response will signal to children what is important. Focusing on spelling and grammar will indicate that correctness is valued above content, whereas focusing on the content by discussing the characteristics of their siblings and comparing these with the ugly sisters, enables the children to become 'critical' readers.

The teaching strategies that are used and the texts selected are very powerful transmitters of cultural knowledge and how children construct the task of learning to be literate. In relation to the texts selected, what seems to be critical is the way in which they are used, rather than merely trying to select the 'right' text, because all texts convey values of some sort.

Given that literacy learning is such a complex task, teachers will use a range of different strategies for different purposes according to the needs of the children. However, what seems to be important is that teachers are consciously aware of which strategies they are selecting, why, and how these actions will impact on the children's understanding of what counts as literacy.

Another aspect of decision making is related to recognition of the specific skills, attitudes and knowledge children bring to the classroom. In order to enable children to feel confident in their own abilities, it is important to recognise, value, consolidate and extend the diversity of children's competence through classroom practice.

When planning a language program which will put the suggested strategies from First Steps into practice, based on the knowledge gained through mapping the children's progress through the indicators, it may be useful to consider the following:

– What new ways of using and understanding language do you want children to develop?
– What sort of contexts will enable this development to occur?
– What sort of texts (oral, written, media, dramatic) will facilitate this learning?
– How will children need to be supported in processing these texts?

– What new skills, processing and knowledge might the children need explicit understanding of in order to complete the language task?
– What underlying values and assumptions encompass your literacy program?
– How will the interactions between you and the children facilitate your aims for literacy development?
– How can you help children to monitor their own progress?

Caroline Barratt-Pugh
Judith Rivalland

Teaching Children for whom English is a Second Language

(or children whose language of home differs from that of the teacher)

When teaching children for whom English is a second language it is important to recognise:

• the diversity and richness of experience and expertise that children bring to school

• cultural values and practices that may be different from those of the teacher

• that children need to have the freedom to use their own languages and to code-switch when necessary

• that the context and purpose of each activity needs to make sense to the learner

• that learning needs to be supported through talk and collaborative peer interaction

• that the child may need a range of 'scaffolds' to support learning and that the degree of support needed will vary over time, context and degree of content complexity

• that children will need time and support so that they do not feel pressured

- that supportive attitudes of peers may need to be actively fostered
- that it may be difficult to assess children's real achievements and that the active involvement of parents will make a great deal of difference, as will on-going monitoring.

Action Research in a wide range of classrooms over a four-year period indicates that effective teaching strategies for children for whom English is a second language and children whose language of home differs from that of the teacher are:

- Modelling
- Sharing
- Joint Construction of Meaning
- The provision of Scaffolds or Frameworks
- Involvement of children in self-monitoring of their achievements
- Open Questions

  Open Questions that are part of sharing or joint construction of meaning, e.g. questions such as 'Do you think we should do … or … to make it work?' or 'It was very clever to do that. How did you think of it?', are very helpful. When children are asked closed questions to which teachers already know the answers, such as 'What colour/shape/size is it?', children often feel threatened and tend to withdraw.

These factors are expanded in the 'Supporting Diversity' chapters in First Steps *Reading: Resource Book* and *Oral Language: Resource Book*.

Caroline Barratt-Pugh
Anna Sinclair

Effective Learning: PEWIT

Many factors enhance or inhibit learning. The following factors help children and adults learn effectively. They are reflected in the First Steps Developmental Continua and Resource Books and underpin all the teaching and learning activities.

- Problem-solving
- Embeddedness
- Working memory
- Interaction
- Time

Problem Solving

Effective learning occurs when children and adults are able to modify and extend their understandings in order to make sense of a situation which has challenged them. This is the essence of problem solving. Effective problem solvers are those who can:
- identify a specific concept or skill as one that is posing a problem
- decide to do something about it
- have a go at finding a solution, using a range of strategies
- keep going until they are satisfied that their new understandings or skills provide the solution they have been reaching for.

Children

Children are natural learners. Young children are constantly learning about their environment through interaction, exploration, trial and error and through 'having a go' at things. As a child's world of experience expands, so deeper understandings are constructed. Additional learning is always built upon existing foundations, and existing structures are constantly being adapted to accommodate fresh insights. Children use language to make sense of their world, imposing order on it and endeavouring to control it.

In coming to terms with the spoken and written language:
  (i) children need to see clearly the purposes for talking and listening, reading and writing so that they can adopt goals for themselves
  (ii) children are engaged in problem solving when they explore oral and written language in their environment, in play and in role-play
  (iii) children are problem solving when they attempt to represent the written language on paper
  (iv) children are problem solving when they attempt to represent oral language in print

Teachers

Teachers are faced with a multitude of challenges every day. How can a difficult concept be introduced? How can the classroom be constantly stimulating for children without risking teacher burn-out? How can a different management strategy be implemented without risk of losing control? How can new insights into gender equity be incorporated into the curriculum?

In implementing change, it is helpful if each challenge can be represented as a problem which can be solved using the technique of 'having a go'; trying out a strategy; reflecting on the result; and then having another go, having slightly modified the strategy, Teachers sometimes expect too much of themselves. They should not expect things to work perfectly first time round. The essence of problem-solving is that strategies and understandings are gradually refined over time. There is seldom one right or easy answer, but a whole range of solutions on a variety of levels that fit the children's needs, teachers' own personal styles and the demands of the tasks.

Embeddedness (Contextualisation)

Most people have had the experience of listening to a speaker and being totally unable to make sense of what is being said. In such circumstances one is apt to say 'I switched off. It didn't make a word of sense.' People need to be able to make connections between their own current understandings and new learning that is being undertaken. A person who knows nothing of mechanics may be quite unable to follow a lecture on car maintenance, but may be able to work things out if the car is there with the bonnet up and the parts clearly visible.

If the context and the problem are embedded in reality and make sense to the learner, then the learner can engage in productive problem solving. If the problem is not embedded in, and seen to be arising from, past experience, then rote learning may occur, but real learning, which is capable of generalisation, will probably not take place.

Children

Children learn effectively in contexts that make sense to them. The challenges which children face and the problems which they attack in their early environment are embedded in familiar, real life contexts. This can be seen quite clearly in early oral language development, when language acquisition is closely tied to the immediate environment and to current needs.

In coming to terms with written language:

(i) children need to be given opportunities to interact with print (read and write) in contexts which make sense to them and which have their counterpart in the real world, in role play and in real situations, e.g. making shopping lists, identifying stop signs

(ii) children need to see adults explicitly modelling reading and writing for a variety of purposes in real situations, e.g. reading and writing notes
(iii) children need to interact not only with books, but with the wide range of print found in daily life, e.g. in newspapers and environmental print.

Teachers

Teachers also need to start from where they are, working within their own familiar context. The First Steps resources offer a number of alternative ways of looking at teaching and a great many strategies and activities which people have found to be useful. Once teachers have decided what problem they want to solve or what challenge they wish to take on, they need to start from a context which makes sense to them and gradually incorporate alternative strategies within their own repertoires. The new learning needs to be embedded within the context of the old and teaching strategies need to be slowly adapted to meet new challenges and different understandings.

Working Memory (Mental Space)

Working memory, which is sometimes called M-space, is very different from long or short term memory. It is, in effect, a measure of the number of discrete elements which the mind can cope with at any one time. A good analogy is that of the juggler, who can juggle competently with four or five balls, but when given one too many, will drop the lot.

Once ideas and skills become familiar as a result of practice over a period of time, two things happen. One is that the learner does not have to think consciously about how to do them any more, so much less space is taken up in the working memory, e.g. spelling a very familiar word. The other is that several different skills gradually become one skill. For example when learning to print children have to manipulate the pencil, remember the formation of letters and consider the order in which the marks have to appear on the page. With practice these individual skills will integrate to become one skill.

Any emotional issue or concern will 'fill up' the mental space more quickly than anything else. Fear, anger or worry may totally inhibit a person's capacity to learn. Most people have had the experience of being unable to concentrate because their mind is fully taken up by an all-consuming emotion. The only thing to do is to give oneself time to 'get it together' again. In the meantime performance on any task will be poor and will continue to deteriorate until the cloud of emotion has lifted. If people say 'I just couldn't think straight', they are usually speaking the truth.

Children

Children focus their entire attention on one element which they perceive to be a challenge. Young children can only cope with one or two different factors at once. As they get older they can juggle with an increasing number of elements, although there is a limit to the amount that anyone can handle.

In coming to terms with the written language:

(i) children may only be able to focus on one or two different factors at any one time. For example, during a shared reading lesson one child may focus on the meaning and spelling of an unusual word in a story, whereas another may be emotionally involved with the characters. Neither may have 'heard' the teacher explaining the use of speech marks.

(ii) as they focus on one skill children may temporarily lose competence in another very familiar skill. For example when a child is absorbed in getting ideas onto paper the quality of handwriting may deteriorate.

(iii) children need to practise and apply a particular aspect of language in a number of contexts until it becomes automatic. Opportunities to practise in stimulating circumstances constitute an important component of all language programs, so that 'mental space' is made available for more complex learning.

(iv) children may appear to make significant regressions if their 'mental space' is fully taken up with an emotional issue relating to home or school.

Teachers

Teachers sometimes make impossible demands on themselves. They are also only able to cope with a certain number of new things at any one time. Instead of attempting everything at once, they need to try one small component of a task first and then build on that. For instance, it is impossible to attempt to observe all the children in a class at once. The secret is to focus on only three or four children a week, looking only at the key indicators. Children thought to be at risk can gradually be placed on the continuum, looking at all indicators.

It is important not to try to do too much at once. If circumstances become overwhelming for any reason, such as trouble at home, too many extraneous duties or ill health, teachers should wait for things to calm down before trying anything new.

Interaction

Interaction is of fundamental importance to human beings. People need to discuss ideas, build on each other's expertise, use each other as sounding boards and work creatively as communities of learners. It is through talk that ideas are generated, refined and extended.

Children

Children need unlimited opportunities to interact with adults and with other children in their daily lives. They need to interact with others to plan, explore, problem-solve, question, discuss and direct their activities. In doing so they try out and modify their ideas. As they use language in social situations they refine their language use and learn more about how language works.

In coming to terms with the written language:

(i) children need freedom to interact with adults in discussions about writing and reading. These discussions should not always be dominated by adults. Children need opportunities to direct conversation. The adult role may be to provide feedback and reinforcement.

(ii) children need freedom to interact with their peers to discuss problems and to formulate and clarify their ideas as they write

(iii) children need to feel safe to ask for help when they need it.

(iv) children need freedom to experiment with written language in socially supportive situations.

Teachers

Teachers also need time and opportunities to interact with their colleagues. Often the most profitable interactions take place informally between staff members who trust and respect each other. Time can also be put aside at a regular meeting for a school staff to discuss and share professional issues and insights regarding the implementation of First Steps or interesting new initiatives being undertaken by different teachers. One school developed a sharing strategy whereby every staff member concentrated on one specific strategy for a week or two, after which all reported back. This school took advantage of the wealth of expertise which is to be found in any staff room.

It is also extremely helpful to interact with parents informally as well as in more formal conferences to share insights about the children. Interacting with children is also of crucial importance, encouraging a two-way process which will enrich both teacher and child as each listens and responds to the other. Conferences between teacher, parent and child as co-members of the community of learners can also be very profitable.

Time

Children

In their everyday lives children have time to construct understandings gradually through inquiry, exploration and problem solving. They also have time to consolidate and integrate these understandings through practice. The amount of time needed to practise new skills and learnings will vary from child to child. Some may need to apply these understandings in only a few situations before they come to terms with them. Others will need to apply the understandings more frequently and in a wider variety of situations before they can begin to generalise and transfer them.

In coming to terms with the written language:

(i) children need opportunities to have regular and on-going involvement in strategies such as shared book experiences, language experience and playing with language, in order to foster their understandings about how the written language works

(ii) children need opportunities to have regular involvement in activities which give them independent practice in their own time, at their own pace, as often as is needed in both reading and writing

Teachers

Teachers need to be as kind to themselves as they are to their children. They need to give themselves time for reflection; time for experimentation and having a go; time to refine and develop strategies already in place; time for sharing with colleagues and parents and time to enjoy their job. Every adult is growing and developing throughout life. Real growth takes time in every sphere of life and development can be enhanced but not hurried. Teachers need to be confident that they are comfortable with the strategies they are implementing and time will be on their side.

Effective Learning: 'The Three Rs'

Adults and children are all learners moving along a continuum. Teachers and children come together as a community of learners. All can benefit from the three Rs:

- Reflecting
- Representing
- Reporting

Reflecting

Children

Children need time to reflect on an experience and on what they have learned from it. Too often they hustle from one learning activity to another, with no time, no space and no structure to help them stand back and think about what they have learned. If they are encouraged to pause and reflect on the insights they have gained and on things that have suddenly started to make sense to them, they will consciously take control of their learning in a new way. They will develop an awareness of specific understandings and the place of those understandings in the overall scheme of things. They will come to value and respect themselves as learners and will become aware of their own learning processes.

Teachers

Teachers need to take time to reflect on their teaching practice. They need to congratulate themselves on their many successes, to consider their goals and take stock of their current situation. Studies have shown, for instance, that almost all primary school teachers firmly believe in developmental learning, but this is not always reflected in their approach to teaching. Teachers may reflect on their teaching practice by asking themselves questions such as: Are my beliefs and theoretical understandings reflected in my current classroom practice? Are the needs of all children being met? Are children engaged in active learning? Are they interacting effectively with others?

It is always worth taking time to reflect on the reality of daily classroom experience, to analyse strengths and to pin-point the areas that may need extra attention. Management strategies, interaction with parents, collaborative work with other staff members and teacher's own professional development are all areas which can provide food for thought from time to time.

Representing

Children

Children may need to represent their learning in a very concrete form. This may be by drawing a picture, constructing a diagram or by writing down their thoughts. In some learning areas such as maths or science it may involve constructing a model.

Teachers

Teachers may need to clarify their reflections by listing one or two items that seem to be significant. Even if no action is taken immediately, an insight will have been captured and recorded for future use. If an idea is written down it is likely to become a reality.

Reporting

Children

Children need to clarify their understandings by talking about them. Children refine, consolidate and extend their learning by reporting on what they know to a peer, a small group or their teacher. This type of reporting occurs best in a natural context when a child is not under any stress and does not feel 'on show.'

Teachers

Teachers may wish to contribute to the process of school planning by reporting on what they consider to be essential goals, strategies and issues for their schools and their students. Every staff member has a crucial contribution to make which will enrich and extend the operations of the school community. Too often the richness and depth of a teacher's experience is confined to one classroom instead of being available for all members of the educational community. All teachers need the support of every other teacher if children are to gain the full benefit of growing up in a community of learners.

Part II

About Oral Language

This section provides some general information about oral language in the First Steps Program.

Particular emphasis is placed on explaining that the Oral Language Developmental Continuum has been designed to help children develop the 'language of school', and on how to support children whose 'home' language is not English or is different from that of the teacher.

'About Oral Language' includes:

- **Effective Communication**

- **The Oral Language Developmental Continuum**

- **How to use the Oral Language Developmental Continuum**
  - Predict
  - Collect Data
  - Involve parents and children
  - Link Assessment with Teaching
  - Monitor Progress

- **Oral Language Assessment for Children Whose 'Language of Home' Differs from That of the Teacher**

EFFECTIVE COMMUNICATION

EFFECTIVE COMMUNICATION can be achieved by focusing on activities based on purposeful language interactions. Purposeful talk is one of the major means through which children construct and refine their understandings of language. Talk should underpin all language activities.

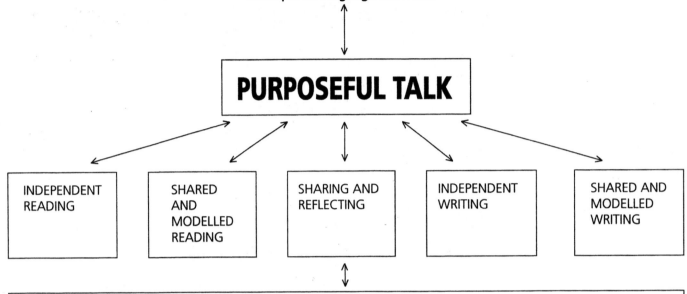

PURPOSEFUL TALK

| INDEPENDENT READING | SHARED AND MODELLED READING | SHARING AND REFLECTING | INDEPENDENT WRITING | SHARED AND MODELLED WRITING |

PURPOSEFUL TALK

Communication occurs when the speaker has effectively relayed his/her meaning to the listener.

Provide opportunities for:
- discussion across the curriculum;
- negotiation;
- group interaction;
- brainstorming;
- clarification of values and issues;
- reflective response to own and others' contributions;
- reading and retelling;
- storytelling;
- news telling;
- drama;
- reporting;
- debating and arguing;
- questioning and enquiring.

PURPOSEFUL WRITING

Communication occurs when the writer has effectively relayed his/her meaning to the reader.
Good spelling is a factor in effectively relaying meaning.

Provide opportunities for:
- learning about writing;
- learning through writing;
- analysing different forms in written context;
- modelled writing;
- editing;
- writing for different purposes and audiences; and
- self evaluation of writing development.

Encourage children to develop spelling skills through:
- word study activities, e.g. derivations, origins, morphemic units;
- visual patterning activities;
- identifying critical features of words;
- using spelling resources;
- word sorting;
- use of personal lists;
- proof reading;
- a range of strategies.

PURPOSEFUL READING

Effective communication occurs when a reader creates, interprets and analyses meanings from text.

Provide opportunities for:
- reading for a wide range of purposes;
- reading a wide variety of different text-types;
- critical reflection on and response to texts;
- discussion which encompasses different interpretations of and responses to text.

The Oral Language Developmental Continuum

The Oral Language Developmental Continuum has been designed to help children come to terms with, and use effectively, the 'language of school'. Most children are competent and effective in their use of oral language at home and in the context of their own community. Experience has shown, however, that if children are to achieve success at school, they need to control the specialised 'language of school'. School language is no better or worse than any other form of language, but it may often seem to be very different and alien to children who are not used to it. A simple example may suffice. Teachers may say 'All eyes on me' when they want children to look at them. They may say 'Everyone sitting up straight' when the children are lounging about and they want them to sit up straight. Such utterances must seem very strange and nonsensical to a young child who has not encountered them before.

When the Oral Language Developmental Continuum was first constructed, an attempt was made to synthesise much of the very considerable research into language development. This original Continuum, although valid in research terms, was found not to be a great deal of use to classroom teachers. The spectrum of oral language is so wide and complex that it seemed to be impossible to contain it within an average classroom. Teachers reported that children did not exhibit many of the indicators in their classrooms and assessment was found to be too difficult. In this current version of the Continuum the decision was made to focus on behaviours pertaining to school-based language that would be evident in the classroom. Teachers decided that their task is to ensure that children are able to use language effectively in school situations and in contexts that society judges essential for success, such as job interviews, discussion, argument, negotiation, etc.

It is hoped, therefore, that the overall pattern of oral language development has been captured as it relates to the context of the classroom and that this has been linked to teaching strategies that will help children succeed within this context. The Continuum is not intended to provide a comprehensive and inclusive picture of the development of phonology, syntax, morphology, semantics and pragmatics.

How to Use the Oral Language Developmental Continuum

- **Predict** where the children are on the Continuum by looking at the Key Indicators.
- **Collect Data** to confirm the prediction, through observation
- **Involve** parents and children
- **Link Assessment with Teaching** by referring to the major teaching emphases
- **Monitor Progress** by ongoing collection of data, consultation with parents and linking children's current phase of development with teaching

Predict

- Read through the Overview of the Oral Language Developmental Continuum, with special reference to the Phase Descriptions and Key Indicators.
- Match your knowledge of the children in your class with the Phase Descriptions and Key Indicators to predict in which phase a child is operating.

Collect Data

The Continuum indicators will help you to gather information about children's oral language behaviours. Your data collection can be carried out when you observe children interacting in the classroom and taking part in regular classroom activities, speaking and listening for a range of purposes and audiences. It is important to give children opportunities for self-evaluation. The *Things I Can Do* checklists starting on page 104 will help children set goals for themselves and monitor their own progress.

Placing Children on the Continuum

- Children are said to be working in a phase when they exhibit *all the Key Indicators* of that phase. However, the placement of a child in a phase must rest upon the teacher's professional judgement.
- For most of the children in a class it is only necessary to look at the Key Indicators.
- If you choose to look at more than the Key Indicators, you will expect and find that children may display behaviours across two or three phases. It is the Key Indicators, however, that determine which phase they are in. The placement in a phase is designed to inform and guide the teaching program.
- For children who come from different cultural and linguistic backgrounds it is inappropriate to use the Oral

Language Developmental Continuum (see pages 18–19). The *Oral Language: Resource Book* offers teaching sequences accompanied by checklists to help teachers ensure that children control the 'language of school' and to monitor their growth in that genre. It is essential that teachers do not judge a student's cognitive or linguistic development by making judgements about performance in English (see chapter entitled 'Supporting Diversity Through Oral Language' in the *Oral Language: Resource Book*).

It is of the greatest importance that a child's 'language of home' is accepted and valued at all times and that the child is encouraged to use it whenever she/he wants. It is often helpful and illuminating if a child is encouraged to carry out a task, such as a barrier game, in their 'language of home'.

Involve Parents and Children

Parents will often have a very clear and accurate sense of their children's competencies. They are usually pleased to be asked to comment on what they have observed at home. Including parents in the assessment and monitoring process by asking for their contributions may help you gain an extremely accurate picture of the children.

Children are also keenly interested in their own progress and enjoy using the list of indicators for children entitled *Things I Can Do*.

Once parents are familiar with the Continuum they will be interested in reading the pages of ideas which suggest how they might like to support their children's development at home.

Link Assessment With Teaching

When children are placed into phases, the section entitled Major Teaching Emphases will guide the selection of appropriate teaching strategies and activities. Many of these are described in some detail in this book. Other fundamental and useful teaching strategies are discussed in the accompanying First Steps *Oral Language: Resource Book*.

Monitor Progress

The Developmental Continuum provides a sensitive and accurate means by which progress can be monitored over time. Monitoring involves further observation and data collection. Links will constantly be made between assessment and teaching. The checklists in the *Oral Language: Resource Book* serve the same purpose. The oral language profile sheets at the back of the book may be used to map individual or class progress. As entries are dated and samples kept it is easy to see how a child is progressing. A record of indicators displayed by a child provides an individualised profile which reflects growing understandings and developing skills.

Oral Language Assessment for Children Whose 'Language of Home' Differs From That of the Teacher

Although oral language permeates classroom learning throughout a school day, it is sometimes very difficult to gather sufficient data to assess children with any degree of accuracy. If children are competent and confident in their use of oral language, assessment may be easy, but if children are reluctant to talk, have English as a second language, or appear to be experiencing difficulties because their 'home' language is different from that of the teacher, data gathered may not present an accurate picture of their real competencies.

It may never be appropriate to use the Oral Language Developmental Continuum for second language learners, as development has already taken place in their first language. For this reason it is recommended that teachers approach oral language assessment by deliberately setting up conditions that promote a specific use of language. Having done this, it may take time to reach common understandings of purpose, audience, context and teacher expectations. Only when all these conditions are established and teacher and children are comfortable and confident in their use of talk, can any realistic assessment take place. Subsequently other contexts will engender more data, and so an accurate and sensitive picture of a child's use of 'school' English emerges. In this way teaching, learning and assessment can be integrated.

The *Oral Language: Resource Book* offers a range of practical classroom activities in contexts that lend themselves to assessment of specific uses of oral languages. Activities are set up in which the purpose and audience are understood and in which the language engendered can be readily assessed. Because the assessment is highly focused on particular aspects of language development, 'learning continua' are included in the *Resource Book* to help teachers monitor and support the development of that particular aspect of language.

For ease of use it is recommended that teachers:
- select an area within the field of oral language that they wish to focus upon, i.e. the language of social interaction, the language of thinking or the language of literacy
- scan the relevant section of the *Oral Language: Resource Book*
- choose and implement an activity that is relevant to the children and that fits the classroom program, using the suggested structures and sequences
- use the appropriate assessment pages to monitor progress when the children (and the teacher) are comfortable with the activity and when spontaneous oral language is being generated

- enter data onto the Developmental Continuum if this seems to be appropriate when sufficient data has been gathered across several areas.

Note

- It is inappropriate to use the Oral Language Developmental Continuum to assess children whose first language is not English or Standard Australian English. The progress of these children can be monitored using the Learning Continua which relate to specific teaching/learning contexts as described above. This will ensure that the links between teaching, learning and assessment are integrated and maintained appropriately.
- If a child's first language is different from that of the teacher, the child's actual language competencies may well be underestimated. It can be very illuminating to give the child a task, such as a barrier game to play in the 'language of home'. This will demonstrate a child's actual competency. Teachers are often amazed when they see how very well children operate when they are not inhibited by the constraints of a second language.
- It is crucial that a child's 'language of home' is recognised, accepted and highly valued by teachers and peers, as culture and personal identity are vested in language. The aspects of oral language that have been focused upon in the *Resource Book* have been chosen so that children are supported and can be monitored in the effective use of language for learning and school interaction.

Part III

Phases of Oral Language Development

By scanning the phase descriptions and key indicators on the overview sheet at the beginning of this book, teachers can place children in a phase of the Oral Language Continuum. Placement can be validated by observing children interacting, speaking and listening in the classroom. Part III of this book provides details of each phase, including all indicators and a wide range of appropriate teaching strategies.

Each phase includes:
- a sample of children's language showing specific indicators
- indicators describing children's behaviours
  key indicators are marked ♦ *and written in bold print*

Teaching Notes
- a description of the major teaching emphases
- advice on establishing an environment for speaking and listening
- a range of appropriate strategies and activities under the following headings:
  - Speech Development
  - Language of Social Interaction
  - Language and Literacy
  - Language and Thinking
- a page for parents

Beginning Language

In this phase, children are motivated by a basic need to communicate; to understand and be understood. Language development is influenced by the children's interaction with other language users, by the opportunities they are given to hear and use language and by their immersion in a stimulating, language-rich environment.

All children move through similar stages of development when they are learning their first language. Development is continuous, although the age at which children display language behaviours varies considerably.

Samples of language:

1 word	Dad	
	Mum	
	no	
	dog	

2 words	Play teddy.	related
	Me jump.	to
	Tim eat.	actions
	Daddy car.	concerned
	Me dress.	with
	Sue book.	ownership

2/3 words	Baby on bed.	related to location
	Under table.	of objects
	Dog here, Mum.	usually associated
	Get book.	with increased mobility and
	Bobby hammer.	developing coordination
	More milk.	related to
	Hit again.	recurrence
	Drink again.	
	No more dog.	referring to non-existence
	No shoes!	negative
	Not your cup!	forms

Beginning Language Indicators

The child:

- develops a repertoire of cries to satisfy biological needs
- cries, chuckles, gurgles, coos
- 'babbles' and repeats sound patterns
- constantly plays at making sounds, alone or with others
- recognises human voices
- responds to own name
- uses voice to attract attention
- uses sound to signify emotions, e.g. anger, excitement
- voices many sounds which resemble those of first language, e.g. ma-ma, da-da
- uses non-verbal gestures, e.g. waves
- produces first real words
- co-ordinates gestures and words, e.g. waves and says *Bye*
- uses single words and two-word phrases to convey meaning:
  drink - I want a drink
  go way - Go away
- uses non-verbal communication to support single and two-word utterances:
  drink - points to fridge
- understands more language than can be verbalised
- may overgeneralise word meanings to represent many ideas:
  bed may mean bed, pillow, blanket, going to bed
- has favourite words, e.g. *No! Mine!*
- relates messages which are supported by facial expression or intonation:
  Mummy car! Mummy car?
- may make mispronunciations:
  tu   for cup
  free   for tree
  ress   for dress
  rink   for drink
- mixes words, e.g. *shakemilk* for milkshake
- has control over some functional language, e.g. *in, on, out, down*
- may produce parents' speech sounds without meaning, e.g. in attempting to hold a conversation with a visitor
- understands simple questions
- follows simple directions
- begins to question for information
- engages in language games, e.g. *Round and round the garden, Incy wincy spider.*

For Parents

How can I help my child with speaking and listening?

Children learn to speak well because:
- parents expect them to
- parents help them in special ways, such as simplifying their language, accepting attempts as approximations of success rather than failure and not over-correcting
- parents surround them with talk
- parents allow them to learn like children
- parents provide them with continuous examples of language which children are not expected to learn all at once
- parents value and celebrate each new step in the communication process—a new word, a learned rhyme or the first attempts at conversation.

- Surround your child with language.
- Talk to your child often, responding to and reinforcing attempts to communicate.
- Read to your child and talk about the story and pictures.
- Provide a selection of durable books with clear illustrations or photographs.
- Do things with your child that involve talking together, e.g. playing simple games, packing away toys, going shopping.
- Introduce rhymes and finger plays, e.g. *Humpty Dumpty, Twinkle, Twinkle Little Star, Round and Round the Garden Like a Teddy Bear.*
- Provide a range of toys that encourage exploration and experimentation. Promote language development by talking to and encouraging your child to form ideas and understandings about his/her world, e.g. *Let's build a tall house. It's getting higher. More blocks. Oh, no! What's happened? It's crashed!.*
- Include play equipment such as:
  - blocks
  - soft toys
  - movable toys, e.g. cars, wheels, balls, carts
  - hammering toys
  - cardboard boxes and junk materials
  - sandpit and toys
  - water trough
  - bath toys
  - musical toys.
- Talk with your child, introducing words to describe the shape, colour, movement of toys as you both play with them.

- Solve problems together, e.g. hiding and locating objects, placing shapes in a posting box.
- Read nursery rhymes, sing songs and chant chants to help your child hear the sounds and patterns of language.
- Join a playgroup.
- Enrol in a toy library.

Early Language

PHASE 2

Children's use of language becomes more refined and extended. It is used to satisfy simple social needs and to gain control of objects, people and knowledge in the environment.

Note: Children attending pre-primary or primary school who display Early Language Phase indicators may communicate effectively in their home environment but may have difficulty responding to the language demands of a classroom.

Sample of Newstelling: Steven
(Pre-primary)

Ch: *My dad made a cubby.*
T: *When did he make the cubby?*
Ch: *Today.*
Aud: *When did you paint it?*
Ch: *Yesterday.*
T: *How could you paint it yesterday when you made it today? How could that happen?*
Ch: *Because why? Because we just builded it.*
T: *Did you buy it?*
Ch: *I think. Yesterday.*
Aud: *Where is it?*
Ch: *Near fence.*

From this sample we can assume that Steven:

◆ **uses own grammar style which is an approximation of adult grammar— overgeneralisations are common, e.g. verbs - 'builded' for 'built'**
• may confuse tenses when describing an event
◆ **is more aware of listener needs and begins to provide feedback for information when introducing new topic**
• coordinates gesture and tone of voice to convey meaning
◆ **gives simple descriptions of past events**
◆ **shows an interest in explanations of how and why**
• begins to verbalise reasons
• offers solutions and explanations to a situation

Newstelling requires children to recall, sequence and summarise experiences for presentation to an audience. Steven needed teacher intervention to extend his recount and clarify information for the listener

Early Language Indicators

Speech Development

(See p. 31)

The child:

◆ **uses own grammar style which is an approximation of adult grammar— overgeneralisations are common, e.g.**

plurals	sheeps for sheep
verbs	goed for went
auxiliary verbs	I did run fast

- experiments with sounds through rhyme and repetition
- is beginning to use pronouns but may make errors in syntax, e.g. *Look at the doggie. They is big.*
- shows confusion between pairs of terms, e.g. *I/you, this/that, here/there*
- demonstrates an understanding of distinction in personal pronouns, e.g. *Give it to him. Give it to me.*
- begins to use endings such as *ing, ed, s*
- may confuse tenses when describing an event, e.g. *I going shopping yesterday*
- uses function words—*is, was, a, the, for, because* - to link ideas previously expressed in unconnected ways: *Me go park*—becomes *I'm going to the park*
- demonstrates an understanding of most common prepositions, e.g. *on, under, front, behind*
- may make sound substitutions, e.g.

b for v	*dribe* for drive
t for k	*tick* for kick
s for sh	*sip* for ship
w for r	*wabbit* for rabbit
d for th	*brudda* for brother
f for th	*free* for three

- focuses on interesting sounding words and enjoys repeating them, e.g. *beautiful - bb-oo-di-fool.*

Language of Social Interaction

(see p. 32)

The child:

◆ **is beginning to develop awareness of listener needs and begins to provide feedback information when introducing new topic, e.g. Nanna, I went shopping. Look at this.**

- is aware of social conventions but does not match actions to phrases, e.g. *'scuse me'* and pushes friend with the blocks
- co-ordinates gesture and tone of voice to convey meaning, e.g. *I love you, Mum* (cuddles)
- refines conversation skills, e.g. learns ways to enter conversation, takes turns during an interaction
- talks aloud to self
- engages in imaginary play, often using toys or other props
- converses with imaginary friends.

Language and Literacy

(See p. 33)

The child:

◆ **gives simple descriptions of past events**

- shows an interest in listening to and talking about stories
- asks for and joins in stories
- 'reads' books aloud, often assigning own meaning to print
- tells 'stories' about pictures in books
- begins to develop an understanding of story structure, e.g. notices when a page is not read from a favourite book
- 'pretend reads' to other children, dolls, toys
- retells simple stories
- demonstrates an awareness of rhyme
- reads familiar print in the environment
- acts out stories or repeats phrases encountered in books
- draws symbols and 'reads' the message
- shows an interest in the meaning of words encountered in books.

Language and Thinking

(See p. 34)

The child:

◆ **shows an interest in explanations of how and why**

- is able to express an opinion, e.g. *'I don't like...'*
- is beginning to develop concepts of quantity, size, speed, time
- begins to see relations between objects, e.g. puts toys together, building blocks
- is beginning to understand cause and effect, e.g. *My tower fell over 'cos I put this big block on top*
- begins to verbalise reasons
- makes simple predictions of future events, e.g. *We'll be going in two more sleeps*
- offers solutions and explanations to a situation, e.g. *It sank 'cos it was full*
- expresses feelings
- constantly questions - *why, who, what, where, when*
- may demonstrate confusion between fantasy and reality, e.g. *I didn't break it. Monster did.*

Teaching Notes

Children develop as speakers and listeners through a natural process of growing up, encountering new experiences or relationships and becoming more aware of themselves and others as language users. However, the contrast between the conditions in which children learn language at home and the expectations of language use in the classroom is often dramatically different.

Children attending pre-primary or primary school who display many of the indicators of this phase will need assistance to prepare them for the demands and challenges of formal schooling. For example, some may have a firm grasp of the language of their home environment but may have difficulty communicating at school. They may have a knowledge of language patterns but may not be familiar with the language of literature. Others may have effective communication skills but the way in which they are displayed may not seem appropriate in the classroom. Other children may speak fluently in their first language but may be grappling with the syntax and vocabulary of English.

In the classroom, the *purpose* for speaking and listening places different demands on children to use language in particular ways. Give all children opportunities to become increasingly confident and competent in using language for many purposes across all curriculum areas.

The *audience* with whom children interact influences the type of speaking and listening which occurs in the classroom. In this phase, children should be provided with a wide range of experiences to develop their ability to select and use language appropriately for different audiences in a range of *situations*. It is particularly important for children to interact with teachers and other adults to enable them to listen and respond to a variety of language styles.

Children's knowledge of classroom *topics* or resources influences what they say or how they express themselves. Teachers should introduce activities which provide insights into children's background knowledge, skills and understandings, e.g. their knowledge of a topic, the proficiency with which they use language, the extent of their vocabulary, concept development and thinking processes.

Information gained should be used as a basis for planning and implementing strategies to further extend children's language development and learning.

Major Teaching Emphases

◆ **focus on language structures and patterns through songs, chants, rhymes and stories**
◆ **develop children's ability to adjust their language to suit particular purposes, audiences and situations**

- ◆ **encourage children to tell stories, recount experiences, describe ideas, events and objects, report information and role play characters and situations**
- ◆ **develop and extend children's use of vocabulary in different contexts**
- ◆ **help children to give and receive simple explanations, information and instructions**
- • focus on literacy-related language through shared reading and modelled writing
- • show children how to plan and work collaboratively

At all phases:
- ◆ **provide models of correct English**
- ◆ **ensure that students encounter a range of purposes, audiences and situations that challenge them to use language in many different ways**
- ◆ **allow time to practise the sounds, rhythms, words and structures of language**
- ◆ **make links between oral and written language**
- ◆ **encourage students to respond to a range of oral and visual texts**
- ◆ **value the processes of group interaction.**

◆ *Entries in bold are considered critical to the children's further development.*

Establishing an Environment for Speaking and Listening

Create an environment which promotes active listening and productive talking. Children are more likely to express their understandings and thoughts when they are learning in a caring environment where others listen, show an interest in and value what they say.

Providing a variety of challenging experiences enables children to build upon their existing language strengths. The classroom environment, like the home environment, should promote language as an instrument for learning — for seeking information, expressing ideas, satisfying curiosity, establishing relationships and linking new experiences with past understandings. Children's knowledge about, and understanding and use of language will be extended when they have the opportunity to interact and experiment with a range of language styles across the curriculum. Every experience becomes a potential source of oral language development when children speak and listen for real purposes in an environment which challenges them to extend their language and learning abilities.

Ways to Create an Environment for Speaking and Listening

- Create a classroom which motivates children to speak and interact. Include areas for specific activities, materials, children's interests, small groups, large groups.
- Arrange seating to allow children to explore, create and move around freely.
- Provide a balance between quiet and noisy areas.
- Include tables or boards to display children's items of interest, work samples or topic-related resources. Encourage children to discuss displays with peers.
- Set up a corner for independent activities. Have children share responsibility for the care and storage of materials and equipment.
- Use a varied vocabulary and paraphrase to clarify meaning.

- Encourage spontaneous make-believe and role play. Such experiences provide children with the opportunity to talk through new concepts, relive experiences and experiment with new ideas. Provide a selection of non-specific materials to activate children's imagination, e.g. cardboard boxes, old blankets, rope, steering wheels, blocks, wheels, telephones. Add a dress-up box to store bags, hats, shoes, beads, belts, coats, dresses, trousers, sunglasses, masks.
- Create a puppet corner with a selection of commercial and class-made puppets. Provide a tray of paper, card, glue, scissors and junk materials. Encourage children to produce their own puppets.
- Set up a home corner with commercially-made equipment or items for improvisation. Add environmental print, e.g. calendars, message boards, telephone books. Supply writing materials and model different purposes for writing, e.g. completing shopping lists, writing letters, sending greeting cards.
- Role play with children so they can hear the language used in different contexts e.g. Post Office, Restaurant, Doctor's Surgery, Shop.
- Provide a set of telephones and message pads. Encourage children to ring each other and have-a-go at writing messages. Model language for making or receiving telephone calls.
- Create a shop or shops. Include a supermarket, card shop, newsagent, greengrocer or restaurant. Provide items such as shopping bags, cash register, money, empty food packets, purses, trolleys, scales. Include paper and pencils for writing shopping lists. Introduce new vocabulary by playing description-related or 'What am I?' games.

- Set up a restaurant or fast food outlet. Supply aprons, cutlery, chairs, chef hats, plates, menus, plastic food, money. Add writing materials for making menus or taking orders. Model appropriate vocabulary and behaviours.
- Establish a post office. Model how to write letters, address envelopes, complete greeting cards. Display samples of letters, postcards, etc. Allocate a time for emptying the letterbox and delivering mail.

- Set up a hospital, doctor's or dentist's surgery. Make an ambulance and beds from boxes or blocks. Add blankets, bottles, bandages, bowls, cotton wool, doctor's coat, nurse's uniform, dolls, telephone and prescription pads. Introduce appropriate vocabulary and conduct role-play sessions to extend children's use of language in different situations.
- Make a prop box to provide opportunities for role play after outings or visits by community members. Display charts, posters or subject-related books.
- Integrate drama activities in music, storytelling and curriculum-related topics. Plan activities for individual enjoyment rather than for an audience. Model how language and vocabulary can express feelings, communicate ideas, recall experiences or narrate stories. Involve children in making props and puppets for dramatic activities.
- Teach nursery rhymes, finger plays, counting rhymes and alphabet chants.
- Introduce a variety of music-related activities such as singing, chanting, experimenting with instruments, listening and moving to music.
- Provide a cassette recorder or listening post and include a selection of stories, songs or rhymes.
- Talk about the weather and record daily information on a chart.
- Provide a wide and balanced selection of books. Model reading behaviour and draw attention to features of print. Encourage children to ask and answer questions.
- Include time for literature-related activities. Tell stories, invite storytellers or readers and encourage older children to visit and read stories.
- Set up a reading corner which includes a range of styles, formats, print, illustrations and quality of books. Encourage children to bring favourite books from home to share with the class.

- Read predictable books that demonstrate the patterns and rhythms of the English language. Encourage children to join in and predict the next line or event.
- Share class news. Model how to reflect on an experience, select the key elements and present the information in a logical sequence.
- Set routines at the beginning of the year and build upon them. Promote social skills and effective interaction by discussing appropriate and inappropriate behaviour.
- Establish outdoor areas as part of the learning environment. Include interest areas, different heights and surfaces, a sandpit, woodwork benches, fixed and portable climbing equipment, and multi-purpose equipment that children can rearrange.
- Involve children in activities that investigate scientific concepts, e.g. change of state—building mud pies, making ice blocks; cooking and forms of energy, heat, light.

Speech Development

(See p. 26)

It is common for children at this phase of development to overgeneralise rules, particularly past tense forms. These approximations indicate children's awareness of rules and their ability to generalise from what they know. It is part of their normal language development. The language features displayed indicate their attempts to develop rules that govern adult speech.

In responding to children's speech, teachers initially should concentrate on the meaning of the message, rather than listening primarily for the language structures or the way the message is being expressed. At this stage, children should be encouraged to experiment freely with language and express their ideas and understandings confidently. Teachers should reassure children and encourage all attempts to communicate. *Children who are anxious about the 'correctness' of their talking may become reluctant to join in conversations.*

- Recognise that errors and non-standard language are common behaviours in children experimenting and taking risks with language.
- Avoid interrupting unnecessarily as it may interfere with children's train of thought.
- Try to avoid predicting what children are going to say and doing the talking for them.
- Provide opportunities for children to hear and practise different styles of language in a variety of real situations, e.g. talking to peers, teachers, other adults, visitors.
- When children use language appropriate to the developmental phase but not yet in the adult form:
  – introduce alternatives incidentally without forcing attention away from the **meaning** of what is being said
  – provide and structure opportunities in which children hear and practise a variety of forms of language in a variety of situations
- When children consistently use forms that may seem immature, repeat the utterance using an alternative form. For example:
  Child: *I did went there.*
  Teacher: *Yes, you went there.*
  Do not pursue the matter further, children will benefit from models of language use when they are ready to and not before.
- Introduce chants and music where repetitive language is a feature. Use clapping and percussion instruments to highlight the rhythm and sounds of the language.
- Have fun with language by introducing finger plays, action rhymes and nursery rhymes. Participating in familiar chants develops confidence and provides practice in repetitive language patterns. This supports children in reading and writing development.

- Introduce speech rhymes that focus on particular sounds. Tape the rhymes and provide a listening post or cassette recorder. This activity may help a child develop the phonetic awareness that will be of use in later reading and writing activities.
- Sing along with taped songs. Encourage children to sing during other class activities, e.g. in free play, on the climbing equipment, during drama sessions.
- Provide puppets and model how to use language in different situations, e.g. requesting information, relaying a message, describing an object, recounting an experience. Have children role play different characters using language for different purposes.
- Develop communication skills by asking children to relay messages or information to other children, other teachers, parents or visitors.
- Support children's responses and expressions as worthwhile attempts to communicate meaning.
- Rephrase questions or provide additional background information to promote further understanding.
- Make links between familiar home experiences and language experiences organised in the classroom, e.g. cooking, telephoning, planning parties, preparing for visitors.
- Provide materials that children may already have at home, e.g. Lego blocks, jigsaw puzzles, games etc. Encourage them to share their knowledge or skill with other children.
- Encourage children to contribute to class displays by bringing along books, toys, photos etc.
- Provide opportunities for real-life experiences, e.g. visits to a library, pet shop, fire station, shopping centre, museum, park. Take photos for a class book. Organise activities where children work with a partner to complete a task. The negotiation and cooperation required to work collaboratively will ensure that talk is purposeful and directed.
- Involve children in drama or role-play activities.

Language of Social Interaction

(see p. 26)
Language plays a vital role in the social development of children as they speak and listen to gain an understanding of themselves and others. Children use language to explore relationships, develop communication skills and gain an understanding of how their world functions. The classroom should provide an environment in which children are encouraged to establish friendships, talk, share materials and ideas, and show respect and consideration for others.

The *Oral Language: Resource Book* chapter *Language of Social Interaction* outlines strategies and activities that assist children to adapt language for many purposes and audiences.

The following activities will assist children to develop appropriate and effective communication skills.

- Conversation. Introduce topics and resources that encourage children to engage in spontaneous interaction. Involve them in purposeful or directed conversation by introducing topics, displaying pictures, telling stories etc. Ensure that resources are of genuine interest and within the scope of children's experiences. If necessary, model and discuss appropriate social courtesies, e.g. listening to others, asking and responding to questions.
  - Role play conversations related to classroom interest areas, e.g. shopkeeper and customer, waiter and diner, doctor and patient. Teach courteous language and behaviours, e.g. greetings, thank yous, enquiries.
  - Model conversations with puppets and provide opportunities for children to role play courteous behaviours.
  - Assign tasks that children must complete together. Discuss importance of talking, planning together and helping each other.
  - Stimulate conversation through poetry and other literature-based activities. Comment on appreciative listening and courteous participation.
- Discussions. Encourage children to learn acceptable group behaviour by taking turns to speak and listen politely to others.
  - Discuss recent classroom experiences or activities.
  - Take turns around the group to share work samples. Model how to introduce the item and give a simple description. Encourage the audience to comment or ask questions.
  - Introduce partner sharing sessions. Initially, model appropriate language and behaviours through teacher-child sharing. Observe, and comment on, children's attempts to discuss items.

  - Incorporate small-group sharing at the conclusion of activity-based sessions. Introduce subject-specific vocabulary and support children's attempts to share more detailed information.
- Role plays. Provide opportunities for children and teachers to put themselves in someone else's position and speak and behave in an appropriate manner. Base role plays on real or imagined experiences. However, also ensure that children can relate the situation to their background knowledge.
  - Set up a class hospital and role play the doctor, nurse, patient or visitor.
  - Role play appropriate behaviour for buying or selling items in the class shop.
  - Introduce telephone courtesies. Role play how to take a message, send a greeting or conduct a conversation with a friend.
  - Discuss class rules and role play scenarios, e.g. asking to join in a game, resolving simple conflicts, thanking a peer for sharing.
  - Role play giving or receiving messages.
  - Discuss characters in familiar books. Role play inappropriate behaviours and suggest solutions, e.g. dramatise the lazy animals in *The Little Red Hen*.
- News sessions. Conduct news sessions and discuss appropriate behaviour for speakers and listeners. If necessary, model how to present a simple news item, demonstrating how to think about the experience, select the most important features and present the information in a logical manner for the audience. Comment on appreciative listening and courteous behaviour.
- Use a shared experience to model how to present a news item. Children can identify and relate to information that is included and that which is left out.
- Encourage children to bring along items for 'Show and Tell'. Discuss the speaker's role in displaying and describing the object appropriately. In addition, involve the listeners in commenting or questioning the speaker. (The First Steps Module *Literacy-related Skills* outlines strategies for developing newstelling skills.)

Language and Literacy

(See p. 26)

Provide an environment that enables children to use language as often as possible in a variety of situations with a wide range of people. Success in speaking and listening provides a sound basis for reading and writing. As reading and writing develop, understanding of the written language will enhance speaking and listening.

The *Oral Language: Resource Book* chapter *Language and Literacy* outlines strategies for developing the language of literacy.

- Provide a wide range of interesting and stimulating books that expose children to the structures and language features of written texts.
- Read to children and with children. Allow individuals to select a favourite book and share a reading time alone with the teacher, aide or parent. For example, the teacher may begin reading while the child listens. The child is encouraged to join in and 'read along' during repetitive sections.
- Discuss stories and monitor the children's developing awareness of print. Do the children:
    - listen and talk effectively?
    - ask questions about the text?
    - understand the storyline?
    - listen to and add to others' comments?
    - contribute to discussions?
- Plan activities that develop an understanding of the structure and language of stories:
    - discuss illustrations in books and encourage children to 'tell the story' from the pictures.
    - read predictable texts and encourage children to become involved in the rhyme, rhythm and repetition.
    - read from big books so children can follow the print and join in during familiar sections.

- Identify listening activities that the children enjoy, e.g. poems, rhymes, finger plays, counting rhymes, stories, music. Make charts of favourite rhymes, nursery rhymes, chants. Display and draw attention to the texts as the children recite the rhymes.
- Motivate children to have fun with language, e.g. dramatising, reciting nursery rhymes, nonsense rhymes, jingles or simple poems.

- Establish a reading corner and encourage children to read and discuss books with teachers, aides, parents and peers.
- Collect a series of simple pictures that can tell a story and encourage children to create their own versions.
- Prepare sets of sequence pictures that tell a story or illustrate a logical series of actions.
- Develop observation skills by discussing children's paintings, models, artwork.
- Display two simple pictures that have slight differences. Ask children to discover and describe variations.
- Do jigsaw puzzles and construct models.
- Sort and classify objects, pictures, photographs, shapes, junk materials. Encourage children to explain reasons for choosing particular criteria.
- Discuss classroom events and school experiences.
- Share class news.
- Establish a language-rich environment:
    - set up a writing centre with a variety of papers, pencils and crayons. Include a display board for the children's samples
    - display children's photos and attach name cards
    - display a calendar and point out days of the week
    - make a birthday chart.

- Have teachers, aides and parents write for different purposes in front of the children, e.g. letters, notes, news, messages, rhymes, stories. Motivate the children to have-a-go at writing similar texts during role-play activities.
- Watch TV and Video versions of stories previously read. Discuss similarities and differences in plot, characters etc. and children's preferences.

Language and Thinking

(See p. 26)

Language used to express, reshape and clarify thoughts differs from talk that is more planned and organised. At this stage, teachers need to provide opportunities for children to use language spontaneously as they interact with others to explore new knowledge, create new meanings and talk their way to understanding.

The *Oral Language: Resource Book* chapter *Language and Thinking* outlines strategies and activities for developing cognitive skills.

- Enhance children's critical thinking skills by refraining from providing answers unnecessarily. Rather, ask the children to suggest possible answers or alternatives before offering information.
- Provide open-ended group games that encourage cooperation and interaction, e.g. 'What's the time, Mr Wolf' and Chinese whispers.
- Motivate children to show curiosity in the natural and physical environment. Develop science skills related to observing, manipulating, talking, listening, estimating, classifying, comparing, contrasting, implementing, predicting:
  - grow seeds and develop a garden. Encourage children to ask questions, describe, explain, share observations, predict
  - study animals in the classroom and motivate children to observe, show an interest in similarities and differences, classify physical characteristics.
  - set up experiments to investigate change of state, e.g. ice melting/water freezing, creaming butter and sugar.

- Organise activities that motivate children to find solutions to questions:
  - how can we look after the guinea pigs?
  - why do our shadows become longer or shorter?
  - why is the tadpole's tail shrinking?
- Provide a wide selection of commercial and junk materials that motivate children to experiment, discover, manipulate and express their understandings.
- Include mathematics materials that motivate spontaneous talking during activities. Encourage children to experiment, match, sort, order, build, predict, hypothesise:
  - sort objects using one criterion or several criteria. Introduce relevant vocabulary such as *colour, size, shape, number, use, length, surface, texture*
  - discuss children's choice of criteria, e.g. *colour, size*
  - make patterns based on shape, size, number, etc.
  - challenge children to estimate numbers, sizes or lengths
  - compare numbers, sizes, lengths, heights.
- Introduce mathematical language and provide opportunities for children to use mathematical terms during classroom interactions.
- Plan classroom activities or excursions together. Involve the children in using language to plan, predict, and problem solve. Record information in repetitive language phrases, e.g. *Our Trip to the Zoo*:
  - Planning
    Who'll be going?
    'I'll be going,' said …
    'I'll be going,' said …
  - Predicting
    'I think I'll see a lion,' said …
    'I think I'll see a zebra,' said …
  - Problem solving
    'If it rains, we'll …'
    'If it's hot, we'll …'
- Model how to ask questions to clarify or gain information or analyse and explore ideas. Teach children the 'question words'—*when, who, where, what, why*—that elicit different types of information. Introduce activities that motivate children to ask questions:

- include problem-solving activities
- display unusual photographs or pictures that promote curiosity
- wait for the children to question rather than providing immediate information.
- Provide opportunities for children to express their feelings:
  - respond to literature and music
  - talk about things that make them sad, happy, frightened
  - express opinions about classroom activities. Display photographs or pictures in which a range of feelings is expressed.
- Allow time for children to develop their ideas through role play, imaginative use of language and drama. Encourage them to engage in spontaneous or informal performances related to real or imagined people, situations or events. Provide a wide range of props such as costumes, everyday clothing, puppets, masks.
- Provide children with opportunities to listen for a variety of purposes. When children have something to listen *for* rather than listen *to*, effective learning takes place:
  - ask questions before a story to provide a focus for listening
  - listen to a story in preparation for a drama activity
  - listen to and carry out a series of directions
  - listen to and convey messages
  - listen to a speaker with the expectation that questions will be asked
  - listen for enjoyment.

For Parents

How can I help my child with speaking and listening?

Children learn to talk because they have a powerful motivation to communicate with people. They learn language not just by observing and copying, but by speaking with others as they attempt to make sense of their world.

- Listen to what your child is saying or trying to say.
- Talk to your child often.
- Provide information on 'how to talk' by valuing what your child says and providing a model of how to communicate, e.g. through initiating and maintaining conversations.
- Talk about familiar things and ensure that your child has a wide range of experiences to talk about.
- Involve your child in plans, e.g. preparing for a shopping trip or holiday.
- If your child gets stuck, help him/her to express what he/she wants to say. Your child will then understand more about language and use it effectively in many situations.
- Read a wide range of books together. Children enjoy the experience and learn to love books and reading. Books provide valuable opportunities to talk together while introducing children to the patterns and sounds of the English language.
- Continue to read 'favourite' books. Repeated readings help children make sense of print.
- Link reading, writing and talking as often as possible. For example, talk about and write a simple shopping list in front of your child. Read it together.
- Say or sing nursery rhymes and action rhymes with your child.
- Encourage your child to talk with other children. This will provide opportunities to interact with different models of language.
- Provide an example of good listening and avoid responding with 'Mmm' or 'Just a minute'.
- Talk about topics of mutual interest with the expectation that your child will listen and respond.
- Write as you or your child dictates to show relationship between written and spoken word.
  Model standard speech by repeating a phrase using an acceptable form. For example:
  Child: *I did went there.*
  Parent: *Yes, you went there.*
  Child: *All gone juice.*
  Parent: *Yes, it's all gone.*

- Provide toys and household materials that help your child learn while stimulating talk. Examples could include:
  – blocks
  – plasticine, dough or modelling clay
  – dolls and soft toys
  – movable toys, e.g. cars, balls, bikes
  – jigsaws, e.g. inset boards, posting boxes
  – cardboard boxes, cartons
  – dress-up box.
- Create an outside environment that encourages exploration and manipulation:
  – swings
  – sandpit
  – cubbyhouse.
- Play inside and outside games.
- Enrol in a toy library and book library.

Exploratory Language

In this phase, children already know a great deal about language. They use language competently and include most grammatical patterns. They know that language can be used to express meaning and share experiences with others.

Sample of interaction during free activity time (Pre-primary)

Susan: *'Scuse me, Carol. I need those blocks.*
Carol: *I need 'em too. Have some others.*
Susan: *Well, if you give them here I'll make something good, OK? That's a good idea.*

During this interaction the teacher was observing Susan's social behaviours. (See *Language of Social Interaction* indicators.)

Sample of interaction during a construction activity

Susan: *Put the Lego man on top of the blocks. He can be the driver ... No! ... they're too high ... Watch out! (laughter) ... Oh, no ... (crash) ... Oops! Big mistake ... Now, start with a bigger one ... now it can balance ...*

Sample of newstelling: Susan

Susan: *Before, when it was last night, well my dad had to fix the TV aerial 'cos it kept moving.*
Teacher: *Where was the aerial?*
Susan: *On the roof.*
Teacher: *Is it a flat roof or a pointy roof?*
Susan: *No, it would be all right if it was a flat roof 'cos then you wouldn't slip off 'cos if you have a pointy roof you can slip down. You have to be very careful...*

During newstelling the teacher was observing Susan's effectiveness in recalling an experience and presenting information to an audience. (See *Language and Literacy* indicators.)

During this activity the teacher focused on language that demonstrated how Susan was thinking and solving problems. (See *Language and Thinking* indicators.)

Assessing Susan's Oral Language

- ◆ **has grasped most grammatical rules but may still overgeneralise, e.g. tenses**
- • uses more lengthy and complex sentences
- • uses grammatical connectives to string ideas together, tending to overuse *and, then*
- ◆ **adapts language for social control, requests and for seeking information**
- • sustains one-to-one conversation with children and adults
- • begins to use polite conversational conventions, e.g. *Excuse me*
- • uses language to describe objects, events and feelings
- ◆ **includes when, who, where, what in recounts**
- ◆ **uses language to explain, enquire and compare**
- • shows an understanding of cause and effect

Susan, age 5, exhibits all Key Indicators from the *Exploratory Language* phase. Information was obtained by observing and interacting with Susan during a range of spontaneous and planned classroom activities.

Exploratory Language Indicators

Speech Development
(See p. 43)

The child:

◆ **has grasped most grammatical rules but may still overgeneralise, e.g.**

tenses	**swimmed for swam, keept for kept**
plurals	**mouses for mice**
pronouns	**they put the book in there**

- may still produce non-fluent speech
- may make minor mispronunciations, e.g. *s/w* for th, *fw* for sw
- uses more lengthy and complex sentences, tending to overuse *and, then*.

Language of Social Interaction
(See p. 44)

The child:

◆ **contributes appropriately to classroom interactions, showing or expressing puzzlement if something is not understood**

◆ **adapts language for social control, requests and for seeking information**

- is aware of the impact of language in conflict situations. Often uses adults to deal with conflict
- sustains one-to-one conversation with children and adults
- takes conversational turns as speaker and listener
- is beginning to use polite conversational conventions, e.g. *Excuse me*
- can only see one course of action when in conflict, e.g. *I want that pen*.

Language and Literacy
(See p. 46)

The child:

◆ **includes when, who, where, what in recounts**

- uses language to describe objects, events and feelings
- is beginning to develop a vocabulary for language concepts, e.g. 'sound', 'word', 'sentence'
- engages in imaginative play, using language to negotiate roles, scenes and maintenance of play
- distinguishes between, and describes, past and present experiences
- relates stories from a sequence of 2-4 pictures
- uses story language, e.g. *Once upon a time...*
- may combine fantasy and reality when describing or retelling
- initiates and joins in playground chants and rhymes.

Language and Thinking
(See p. 47)

The child:

◆ **uses language to explain, enquire and compare**

- makes inferences, e.g. *I can't play outside if it's raining*
- describes words in terms of function, e.g. *You ride a horse, You drive a car*
- may display confusion when using pairs of comparative terms, e.g. *more/less, big/little*
- projects into the future, anticipates and predicts, e.g. *If you blow that balloon up any more, it'll burst* or *When we go on holiday we'll need...*
- discusses events, concepts of objects not experienced
- suggests possible alternatives when problem-solving, e.g. *If we use that cardboard box instead of the wood, we'd be able to bend it*
- shows an understanding of cause and effect
- constantly questions
- reflects on own and others' feelings, e.g. *I got mad at Nathan when he took my toys* or *It makes you sad, does it, Mum?*

Teaching Notes

In this phase, children already know a great deal about language. They have considerable confidence when speaking and listening, and bring a wealth of experience and language understandings from home. They use language competently to communicate, socialise and learn. They know that language can be used to express meaning, share ideas and relate experiences. Children also know that language has a function in achieving what they want. It helps them to establish relationships, explain, enquire, create imaginary words or express feelings.

Provide many *purposes* for using language. For example:
- to initiate, explore and maintain relationships
- to provide or request information
- to describe or explain experiences or ideas
- to predict and make comparison
- to clarify thoughts
- to amuse or entertain.

Give children opportunities to interact with a variety of *audiences*. Such experiences will enable them to select and use language appropriate to a range of situations.

Encourage children to interact with different adults in one-to-one or group *situations*. By hearing and responding to different models of language, they will begin to extend and refine their own language repertoire.

Introduce subject-specific vocabulary and provide opportunities for practice through discussions, recounts, descriptions, explanations and role play. Focus on the language of literacy by telling, reading and sharing stories. Model reading and writing behaviours, and demonstrate how oral language can be recorded in print and access to it gained through reading. Discuss the differences between written and oral language.

Encourage children to have fun with language and develop a positive attitude to speaking and listening.

Major Teaching Emphases

- ◆ focus on language structures and patterns through songs, chants, rhymes and stories
- ◆ provide opportunities to develop language through small-group and large-group interaction
- ◆ help children to learn through speaking and listening, e.g. formulating ideas, classifying, comparing, giving and receiving instructions and explanations
- ◆ provide opportunities to retell stories
- ◆ assist children to recount experiences, within and outside school
- ◆ encourage children to talk about reading and writing experiences

◆ **incorporate collaborative and exploratory activities in all curriculum areas**
- encourage children to listen and respond to stories, songs and poems
- engage children in role play and improvised drama
- promote the language of literacy through shared reading and modelled writing
- develop and extend children's use of vocabulary
- develop children's ability to ask and answer questions

At all phases:
◆ **provide models of correct English**
◆ **ensure that students encounter a range of purposes, audiences and situations that challenge them to use language in many different ways**
◆ **allow time to practise the sounds, rhythms, words and structures of language**
◆ **make links between oral and written language**
◆ **encourage students to respond to a range of oral and visual treats**
◆ **value the processes of group interaction.**

◆ *Entries in bold are considered critical to the children's further development.*

Establishing an Environment for Speaking and Listening

Teachers should aim to provide an environment which challenges children to build upon their language capabilities while communicating for real purposes. In an accepting and supportive classroom in which they are encouraged to express their ideas, children will be more willing to take risks and experiment with language. They will be motivated to learn about language — the way it functions, its patterns and organisation — as they hear it being used and use it themselves.

Any growth in learning and language development requires an extension of children's experiences. These experiences should evolve from whole-class, small-group and partner activities in which children are encouraged to work cooperatively, exchange ideas and communicate their discoveries to others. It is primarily through active engagement in speaking and listening experiences that effective learning takes place.

Ways to Create an Environment for Speaking and Listening

- Consider the classroom as an environment for encouraging oral language development. Organise situations and activities in which children can:
  - work with other children to discuss, listen to and exchange ideas
  - develop speaking and listening skills
  - have direct experiences
  - learn from others who have had different experiences
  - find answers to their own questions
  - talk about how they learn.
- Create a classroom that motivates children to speak and interact. Include areas for specific activities, materials, children's interests, small groups, large groups.
- Include an area for the whole class to gather for sharing ideas, discussions and stories. Display books, poem boxes, an easel for holding big books, etc.
- Arrange seating to allow children to explore, create and move around freely.
- Include tables or boards to display children's items of interest, work samples or topic-related resources. Encourage children to discuss displays with peers.
- Set up a corner for independent activities that will stimulate conversation and discussion. Have children share responsibility for the care and storage of materials and equipment.
- Provide a balance between quiet and noisy areas, e.g. a quiet reading corner and a construction or role-play area.

- Encourage spontaneous make-believe and role play. Such experiences provide children with opportunities to talk through new concepts, relive experiences and experiment with new ideas. Include a selection of non-specific materials to activate children's imagination, e.g. cardboard boxes, old blankets, rope, steering wheels, blocks, wheels, telephones. Add a dress-up box to store bags, hats, shoes, beads, belts, coats, dresses, trousers, sunglasses, masks.
- Create a puppet corner with a selection of commercial and class-made puppets. Provide a tray of paper, card, glue, scissors and junk materials. Encourage children to produce their own puppets.
- Set up a home corner with commercially-made equipment or items for improvisation. Add environmental print, e.g. calendars, message boards, telephone books. Supply writing materials and model different purposes for writing, e.g. completing shopping lists, writing letters, sending greeting cards.
- Provide a set of telephones and message pads. Encourage children to ring each other and have-a-go at writing messages. Model language for making or receiving telephone calls.

- Create a shop or shops. Include a supermarket, card shop, newsagent, greengrocer or restaurant. Provide items such as shopping bags, cash register, money, empty food packets, purses, trolleys, scales. Include paper and pencils for writing shopping lists. Introduce new vocabulary by playing description-related or 'What am I?' games.
- Set up a restaurant or fast food outlet. Supply aprons, cutlery, chairs, chef hats, plates, menus, plastic food, money. Add writing materials for making menus or taking orders. Model appropriate vocabulary, language and behaviours.
- Establish a post office. Model how to write letters, address envelopes, complete greeting cards. Display samples of letters, postcards, etc. Allocate a time for emptying the letterbox and delivering mail.
- Set up a hospital, doctor's or dentist's surgery. Supply boxes or blocks for the ambulance. Add blankets, bottles, bandages, bowls, cotton wool, doctor's coat, nurse's uniform, dolls, telephone and prescription pads. Introduce appropriate vocabulary and conduct role-play sessions to extend children's use of language in different situations.
- Make a prop box to provide opportunities for role play after outings, or visits by community members. Display charts, posters or subject-related books.

- Integrate drama activities in music, storytelling and curriculum-related topics. Plan activities for individual enjoyment rather than for an audience. Model how language and vocabulary can express feelings, communicate ideas, recall experiences or narrate stories. Involve children in making props and puppets for dramatic activities.
- Introduce a variety of music-related activities such as singing, chanting, experimenting with instruments, listening and moving to music.
- Teach nursery rhymes, finger plays, counting rhymes and alphabet chants.
- Provide a cassette recorder or listening post with a selection of stories, songs or rhymes.
- Talk about the weather and record daily information on a chart.
- Provide a wide and balanced selection of books. Model reading behaviour and draw attention to features of print. Encourage children to ask and answer questions.
- Include time for literature-related activities. Tell stories, invite storytellers or readers and encourage older children to visit and read stories.
- Set up a reading corner that includes a range of styles, formats, print, illustrations and quality of books. Encourage children to bring favourite books from home to share with the class.
- Read predictable books that demonstrate the patterns and rhythms of the English language. Encourage children to join in and predict the next line or event.
- Share class news. Model how to reflect on an experience, select the key elements and present the information in a logical sequence.
- Set routines at the beginning of the year and build upon them. Promote social skills and effective interaction by discussing appropriate and inappropriate behaviour.
- Establish outdoor areas as part of the learning environment. Include interest areas, different heights and surfaces, a sandpit, woodwork benches, fixed and portable climbing equipment, and multi-purpose equipment that children can rearrange.
- Tell stories without a book, encourage children to join in repetitive phrases.

Speech Development

(See p. 38)

As children practise the sounds, rhythms, words and structures of the English language, they overgeneralise rules, make approximations and gradually modify and refine their understandings of grammar. Practising and experimenting with sound and language patterns is a natural part of language development. Occasions will arise, however, when it is appropriate to intervene to model particular features of children's speech, e.g. pronunciation, syntax or word usage. Any interventions should occur at a time which is meaningful to the children, and in an environment which recognises and respects the language that children bring from home.

In responding to children's speech, teachers initially should concentrate on the meaning of the message rather than the language structures or the way the message is being expressed. Encourage children to practise and experiment with language, express their ideas and opinions, and reflect on the effectiveness of their communication.

- Non-standard speech forms. When children use different forms of language from those of the teacher model a range of alternatives that may be helpful:
  - encourage spontaneous talking through group activities and discussions that place the emphasis on the group rather than the individual, providing a range of models.
  - include activities in which children focus on particular language structures, e.g. choral speaking, singing, assembly items.
  - model standard speech and language forms according to context and purpose. Children learn to speak and listen effectively by interacting with others. The greater the exposure to a range of forms, the sooner children will move towards adult patterns of speech.
- Identify, discuss and role play situations such as:
  - introducing visitors
  - conveying a message
  - speaking at assembly
  - seeking information.
- Avoid interrupting unnecessarily as it may interfere with children's train of thought.
- Focus on meaning, e.g. paraphrase to establish meaning.
- Try to avoid predicting what children are going to say and doing the talking for them.
- Provide opportunities for children to hear and practise different styles of language in a variety of situations, e.g. talking to peers, teachers, other adults, visitors.
- When children consistently use forms of speech that are difficult to understand, introduce alternatives

incidentally without forcing attention away from the **meaning** of what is being said.
- Introduce songs and rhymes where repetitive language is a feature. Use percussion instruments or clapping to highlight rhythms and sounds.
- Sing alphabet songs and jingles.
- Chant repetitive rhymes, nursery rhymes and number rhymes.
- Dramatise nursery rhymes or number rhymes, e.g. *Little Miss Muffet, Two Little Dicky Birds.*
- Have fun with circle games and simple dances, e.g. *Blackbird, The Grand Old Duke of York.* Participating in familiar chants develops confidence and provides practice in a range of language patterns.
- Play games that focus on sounds, e.g. *I Spy.*
- Dramatise traditional tales with repetitive storylines, e.g. *Three Billy Goats Gruff, Little Red Hen.*
- Introduce speech rhymes that focus on particular sounds. Tape the rhymes and provide a cassette and headphones.
- Sing along with taped songs. Include those with simple tunes and language structures.
- Develop an awareness of sounds by experimenting with objects to discover the sounds they can make.
- Provide a range of commercial musical instruments and make class sets from junk materials.
- Use puppets to model how language is used in different situations:
  - requesting information
  - relaying a message
  - describing an object
  - recounting an experience.

Language of Social Interaction

(See p. 38)

Language plays an important role in the personal and social development of children. It helps them explore, establish and maintain relationships. It enables them to share ideas, solve problems together, exchange experiences and show consideration and respect for others.

Children need specific language skills to develop social awareness. They need to know how to communicate effectively and appropriately in a variety of situations. Teachers should provide many opportunities for children to use different styles of language, to adapt these styles to suit a range of purposes and audiences, and to become increasingly more confident in using oral language as a tool for communication.

The *Oral Language: Resource Book* chapter *Language of Social Interaction* provides strategies and activities that assist children to adapt language for many purposes and audiences.

The type of audience influences the style of speaking and listening. In their early years, children interact spontaneously with family and peers. At school, however, they are challenged to adapt and refine language to suit a range of situations and audiences. The following activities assist children to use language for social development.

- Peers. Plan activities both in and out of the classroom, e.g. partner work, peer tutoring, small group discussions.

- Child to teacher. This type of interaction encourages children to question, discuss and reflect on what they are doing. It provides opportunities to listen and respond to adult models of language, and motivates children to use language to extend their thinking. Involve children in activities where they are encouraged to talk, ask questions and express their ideas and opinions.
- Other adults. It is important for children to interact with many adults so they listen and respond to a range of language styles. Introduce other teachers, adults,√ support staff, visitors, parents. Involve them in class or school activities which focus on child-adult interaction, e.g. theme days, interviews, cooking, sport, manipulative activities.

- Small groups. Group size will influence the type of interaction that occurs in the classroom, e.g. children are usually highly motivated to work in friendship groups. To ensure maximum benefit from this type of organisation, include some activities that are sufficiently challenging to extend language use beyond informal chatter.
- Teacher-selected groups. These groups can serve a range of purposes. For example, small-group activities can be organised to focus on a particular skill or strategy. They also provide support for children who lack confidence working in larger groups. Large groups provide a range of language models and require children to respond more formally to a wider audience.

- Discussion. Organise whole-class and small-group discussions in a variety of subject areas. Through discussion, children develop social skills and learn content and vocabulary more thoroughly. They also learn social skills through working with others and developing courteous behaviours. Choose topics related to the children's experiences:
  - home and family
  - pets
  - games
  - school
  - literature
  - classroom activities.

- Conversation. Introduce topics, resource materials, pets, etc. which motivate children to engage in spontaneous conversation. In addition, involve children in purposeful or more directed conversations during subject-related activities. Ensure that the resources are of genuine interest and within the scope of children's experiences. If necessary, model and discuss appropriate social courtesies, e.g. listening to others, asking and responding to questions, showing an interest in what others have to say.

  Use simple activities such as giving out paper and other materials to reinforce importance of saying *please* and *thank you*. Draw children's attention to correct behaviours and reinforce appropriate interactions. Role play conversations related to appropriate and inappropriate behaviour:
  - shopping; buying items or serving customers
  - apologising for rudeness, forgetting, being late
  - listening politely
  - borrowing or returning items
  - greetings; daily greetings, friends, special occasions
  - inviting and accepting invitations
  - asking for permission
  - thanking individuals or groups
  - giving and receiving compliments.

  Model conversation with puppets and encourage children to role play courteous behaviour during spontaneous activities.

  Assign tasks that children must complete together. Discuss importance of talking, planning and helping each other.

  Stimulate conversation through poetry and other literature-based activities. Comment on appreciative listening and courteous participation.
- Explanations. Include explanations in small groups where speakers can receive immediate feedback from peers or adults. Introduce appropriate vocabulary and questions to elicit information, e.g. *What is it?, How did you make it?, Can you tell us what you used?*
- Messages. Provide opportunities to convey messages in meaningful situations. Encourage other staff members to participate in sending and receiving daily messages. Provide practice in listening for information, repeating the message, asking for clarification and speaking clearly. Teach children the courtesies involved in approaching and waiting, interrupting politely and waiting for a reply.
- Telephoning. Provide a set of telephones for the classroom and model correct procedures for making or receiving a call. Encourage children to incorporate telephone activities during role-play sessions.
- Excursions and visits. Direct experiences broaden children's general knowledge and provide opportunities to respond to a range of language styles. Include experiences in the immediate school environment, e.g. library, dental clinic, canteen or administration block. Visit areas of interest in the local neighbourhood, e.g. shops, playground, park, post office, building site, local library. Organise excursions in the wider community, e.g. zoo, museum, theatre, neighbouring school or town. Use the visits to encourage language development through discussion, giving descriptions, sharing information, comparing, recalling and reporting.

Language and Literacy

(See p. 38)

The conditions that encourage children to speak and listen also provide a solid foundation for the development of reading and writing skills. Children need to use oral language to develop their powers of reasoning and observation, prediction, sequencing and other skills connected with reading. They also need to develop an awareness of the connections between oral and written language, i.e. that speech can be written down and read back.

The *Oral Language: Resource Book* chapter *Language and Literacy* outlines strategies and activities for developing literacy understandings through oral language.

- Provide a wide range of interesting and stimulating books that expose children to the structures and language features of written texts.
- Read to children and with children. Allow individuals to select a favourite book and share a reading time alone with the teacher, aide or parent. Encourage the child to 'read along', discuss favourite parts or ask questions.
- Encourage children to take an active part in group storytelling or story-reading.
- Discuss stories and monitor children's developing awareness of print. Do the children:
  - listen and talk effectively about the texts?
  - make predictions?
  - ask questions?
  - understand the story-line?
  - listen to and add to others' comments?
- Introduce shared reading sessions and encourage all children to participate. Repeated experiences with the same favourite texts will help children develop familiarity with the language and structure of stories. Focus on texts with rhyme, rhythm, repetition and predictable story-lines.
- Discuss illustrations in books and encourage children to 'tell the story' from the pictures.
- Introduce a selection of big books that activate a range of responses, e.g. stimulate children's imagination, provoke curiosity, make them laugh, provide information or elicit delight or wonder. Discuss what made them feel a particular way. Talk about the language used in the text to convey different emotions.
- Identify listening activities that the children enjoy, e.g. rhymes, finger plays, songs, counting rhymes, chants. Make charts of favourite rhymes and draw children's attention to the texts.
- Integrate drama activities in storytelling and literature sessions. Encourage children to use 'storybook' language, e.g. *Once upon a time, ... and that was that.*
- Involve children in making puppets or props for story-related drama activities.

- Establish a reading corner, and motivate children to read and discuss books with teachers, aides, parents and peers.
- Collect a series of simple pictures that can tell a story and encourage children to create their own versions.
- Prepare sets of sequence pictures that tell a story or illustrate a logical series of actions.
- Display pairs of pictures that have slight differences. Ask children to discover and describe variations.
- Sort and classify objects, pictures, photographs, shapes, junk materials. Have children talk about their decisions and describe attributes, e.g. size, colour, shape, texture, weight.
- Do jigsaw puzzles and construct models.
- Develop the language of description through games that focus on attributes and function. Sort shapes, complete puzzles, describe objects, play barrier games. Introduce terms related to size, colour, shape, texture, weight and use.
- Organise partner or group activities that challenge the children to talk and work together, e.g. setting up a construction area, reorganising the home corner, tidying the book shelves, building a city from blocks.
- Discuss classroom events and school experiences. Model how to present a simple recount that includes *when, who, where, what.*
- Establish an environment for writing:
  - display alphabet books, letters and friezes
  - display captions around the room
  - set up a writing corner that includes pencils, crayons, felt pens and paper
  - provide purposes for writing, e.g. messages and shopping lists in the home corner, telephone messages at the doctor's surgery
  - include a children's display area
  - provide a postbox, stamps, envelopes, writing paper.
- Model writing in situations that have meaning, e.g. writing class news, making captions, writing a list, taking a message.

Language and Thinking

(See p. 38)

Children in this phase use language to reflect on experiences, predict outcomes and solve problems. They often talk to themselves (aloud or sub-vocally) as they discuss plans and intentions, consider alternative courses of action or make decisions. They constantly question as they search for reasons, causes and outcomes.

Teachers need to organise many experiences that activate children's thinking and motivate them to verbalise their thoughts. Such experiences provide teachers with insights into children's understandings and knowledge. For children, they provide a medium for clarifying thinking, solving problems and linking past experiences to new situations.

The *Oral Language: Resource Book* chapter *Language and Thinking* outlines strategies and activities for developing cognitive skills.

- Problem solving. Children develop thinking skills when they use language to experiment, explore and solve problems. Take time to create situations in the classroom that require children to plan and work cooperatively to complete tasks. The talking that evolves from such activities helps children clarify their thinking, share knowledge and express new understandings:
  – complete jigsaws and puzzles
  – build models to specifications, e.g. tall, wide, two levels
  – conduct experiments
  – use construction materials.

- Partner activities. Introduce shared activities that encourage children to talk together, exchange ideas, express opinions, and reflect on their learning:
  – role play events and situations
  – create puppet plays
  – discuss favourite books
  – complete art and crafts activities.
- Developing curiosity. Motivate children to show curiosity in the natural and physical environment. Develop science skills related to observing, manipulating, talking, listening, estimating, classifying, comparing, contrasting, experimenting, predicting:
  – plant seeds, bulbs and establish small gardens

  – study animals in the classroom and motivate children to observe, show an interest in similarities and differences, classify physical features
  – display rocks, seeds, leaves, bones, fibres and encourage children to compare and describe observed features
  – provide magnifying glasses, magnets, torches, mirrors, simple machines that activate children to question, manipulate and discover.
- Finding solutions. Organise activities that motivate children to find solutions to questions:
  – why are there colours in the puddles where cars have been parked?
  – how does the water pump work?
  – why do the rocks look bigger when you use a magnifying glass?
  – when will the guinea pigs have babies?
- Choosing resources. Provide a wide range of commercial and junk materials that can be manipulated during open-ended activities. Encourage children to talk as they balance, stack, sort, attach and construct.

- Mathematics. Develop mathematical concepts and vocabulary through spontaneous and directed play:
  - involve the children in movement activities to develop understandings of *tall, short, wide, near, far, high, low*
  - make collages using shapes and talk about attributes, patterns, symmetry
  - compare size, length, height, width during construction activities
  - develop logical thinking by sorting, classifying and making sets
  - discuss attributes and introduce specific vocabulary, e.g. *sharp, narrow, long, curved*
  - arrange objects in order of size and discuss features, e.g. *bigger than, smaller than, taller than*
  - look for patterns in the environment.
- Classification. Make classification charts related to curriculum topics. Collect an assortment of relevant pictures and back with strips of adhesive paper or Velcro. Discuss the most appropriate groupings and have children sort under headings. Encourage children to reclassify the pictures during free activities.

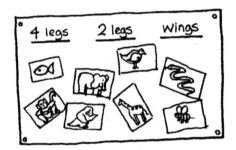

- Planning. Organise classroom activities or excursions together. Involve the children in using language to plan, predict and problem solve. Record information in repetitive language phrases, e.g. *Our Trip to the Circus*:
  - Planning
    'Who's going to the circus?'
    'I'm certainly going,' said …
    'I'm determined to go' said …
  - Predicting
    'Perhaps we'll see a clown'
    'Maybe we'll see an elephant'
    'I'm sure we'll see a juggler'
  - Problem solving
    'How can we get there?'
    'We could catch a bus'
    'We could borrow some cars'
- Questioning. Model how to ask questions to clarify and gain information or analyse and explore ideas. Teach children the question words—*when, who, where, what, why*—that elicit different types of information. Introduce activities that motivate children to ask questions:
  - include problem-solving activities
  - display unusual photographs or items

- read books that challenge children to find solutions
- wait for the children to question rather than providing immediate information.
- Literature. Read books and ask questions that motivate children to think about the text:
  - detail—*what, who, which*
  - sequence—*What happened after …?*
  - cause and effect—*Why did …?*
  - character traits—*What sort of person was …?*
- Expressing feelings. Provide children with opportunities to express their feelings:
  - respond to literature and music
  - talk about things that make them sad, happy, frightened
  - express opinions about people, books, experiences.
  Display photographs that reveal a range of emotions.
- Imaginative play. Allow children time to develop feelings, ideas and understandings through drama, role play and make-believe. Encourage them to engage in spontaneous and directed activities related to music, literature, real or imagined events.
- Listening. Provide children with opportunities to listen for a variety of purposes. When children have something to listen *for*, rather than listen *to*, effective learning will take place:
  - ask questions before a story to provide a focus for listening
  - listen to stories or music in preparation for drama
  - listen to and carry out a series of instructions
  - listen to and convey messages
  - listen to a speaker with the expectation that questions will be asked
  - listen for enjoyment.
- Take opportunities to talk about your own feelings and the reason for them with the children

For Parents

How can I help my child with speaking and listening?

- Observe what your child is doing and support what he/she knows.
- Listen to what your child is saying or trying to say.
- Talk about familiar things and experiences. In addition, provide a wide range of experiences and activities which will motivate your child to share ideas and understandings.
- Help with meaning, e.g. explain the meanings of words, add information to clarify understanding, or paraphrase.
- Establish a story-time routine and read a wide range of books.
- Talk about books, including print and illustrations.
- Provide books for your child to read.
- Read and teach nursery rhymes, finger plays and number rhymes.
- Tell stories such as Hans Andersen's Fairytales or other traditional stories.
- Provide taped stories with read-along books. This is a worthwhile activity linking reading, talking and listening in an enjoyable way. These can be borrowed from the library.
- Provide tapes of stories and songs when travelling.
- Play games that motivate children to learn language, e.g. *I Spy*, rhyming words, finding signs along the road, jokes, riddles etc.

- Provide a dressing-up box with old clothes, shoes and hats.
- Engage in activities that involve talking, writing and reading together, e.g. making a shopping list, doing the shopping, writing a letter, sending a birthday card.
- Encourage your child to tell you about what has been happening.
- Accept and praise your child's attempts to read.
- Ensure that your child sees adults reading.
- Write and display messages, e.g. 'John, collect the letters.'
- Include children in some adult conversations, so that they hear adult language use.
- Provide paper and pencils and encourage children to have-a-go at writing.
- Talk about signs, displays, advertisements etc. in the community.
- Sing alphabet songs and discuss letter names.
- Talk about your child's drawing and writing.
- Develop mathematical language and understandings through counting, sorting, matching and talking about numbers, numerals, shapes, sizes and physical properties.
- Teach your child to use the telephone.
- Join a toy library.
- Enrol in a book library.

Emergent Language for Learning

PHASE 4

In this phase, children use language effectively to satisfy social and communicative needs. They also display considerable skill in responding to, and using language to satisfy, the demands of formal learning.

Sample of newstelling: Gina (Year 2)

… Well, um, I'm going to tell you about when we went to the zoo and all the kids in my group, well, we went to the monkeys and we saw some, um, monkeys that had bare bottoms (giggles)…

… and then one, went, and when me and Alison went, 'Hello, hello', and it went like this (gesture, laughter from audience) and when we went to the other one, the other one went like this (gesture) … really fast 'cos it's much bigger than the other … and stronger and …

… and when I was talking to, um, Justine today about the zoo, um, well she thought I said the crocodiles was in, were in the mountain goats' cage, um, and so then we said if the crocodiles was in, were in the mountain goats' cage they'd eat everything all up … and I'm telling her about the, um, the, er, monkeys, gorillas and, it, it was just giving me a total headache.

Sample of interaction during partner activity

Gina: *Let's sort them first. Which bit's got the hen picture? She planted that stuff … wheat.*

Carol: *Yeah, but she's got the wheelbarrow.*

Gina: *No, yeah, this is it. See … she's got a bag of wheat.*

Carol: *Yeah, put it here. What happened next? Hey! Who took the book …?*

Gina: *No, it's here. Find the page … You find the picture and I'll look at this picture … Can you find it?…*

Assessing Gina's Oral Language

- has grasped most grammatical rules but may still overgeneralise
- ◆ **judges whether a sentence is grammatically correct and adapts accordingly**
- ◆ **takes into account audience and purpose when speaking**
- ◆ **can sustain a conversation with a variety of audiences**
- distinguishes between language used in different situations, e.g. 'home', 'classroom' and 'playground' language
- takes conversational turns as speaker and listener
- ◆ **develops specific vocabulary to suit different purposes, e.g. language for description, classification, comparison, argument**
- ◆ **shows evidence of language cohesion; (b) recounts – sequenced by time order**
- uses language to describe similarities and differences
- uses language to discuss cause and effect
- ◆ **uses language to predict and recall**

Gina, age 7, exhibits all key indicators from the *Emergent Language for Learning* phase. Information was obtained by observing Gina during planned presentations (newstelling) and interactive sessions (partner and group work).

Emergent Language for Learning Indicators

Speech Development

(See p. 56)

The speaker/listener:

◆ **judges whether a sentence is grammatically correct and adapts accordingly**
- has grasped most grammatical rules but may still overgeneralise, e.g.
  - verbs   *sleeped* for slept
  - plurals   *mouses* for mice
- is beginning to use some complex grammatical connectives to sustain a topic, e.g. *because, if, after*
- uses cognitive verbs, e.g. *think, like, want,* etc. to express thoughts, wishes, dreams
- uses slang and jargon with peers.

Language of Social Interaction

(See p. 57)

The speaker/listener:

◆ **uses tone, volume, pace, intonation pattern and gesture to enhance meaning**
◆ **takes into account audience and purpose when speaking**
◆ **can sustain a conversation with a variety of audiences, e.g. teacher, peers, parents**
- takes conversational turns as speaker and listener
- responds to classroom expectations of polite behaviour, e.g. *Could you pass me..., I'm sorry.* Waits for turn before speaking
- participates in group discussions
- distinguishes between language used in different situations, e.g. 'home language', 'classroom language' and 'playground language'.

Language and Literacy

(See p. 59)

The speaker/listener:

◆ **develops specific vocabulary to suit different purposes, e.g. language for description, classification, comparison, argument**
◆ **shows evidence of language cohesion;**
  (a) narrative logical, sequenced retells
  (b) recounts sequenced by time order
  (c) conversation sustained, on topic
- includes *when, who, where, what* in recounts
- shows a knowledge of story structure by describing, comparing or contrasting, setting, characters, events, conclusion, etc. in narrative texts

- uses language to express grammatical forms encountered in narrative texts, e.g. *Once upon a time..., ...and they lived happily ever after*
- engages in more elaborate role play of characters or events encountered in stories.

Language and Thinking

(See p. 62)

The speaker/listener:

◆ **uses language to predict and recall**
◆ **uses language to interact with peers, e.g. collaborative activities**
- demonstrates abstract thinking by using verbs of cognition to express thoughts, hypotheses, wishes, e.g. *I wonder, hope, understand, think, believe, wish*
- uses language to describe similarities and differences
- uses language to categorise objects, people, places, events, etc.
- uses language to discuss cause and effect
- uses language to reason and argue
- is beginning to distinguish between language forms and language meanings, e.g. *Pull your socks up* means *Improve your behaviour*
- is beginning to understand humour in jokes and riddles
- follows instructions, e.g. classroom routines, relaying messages
- plans and gives instructions in a variety of situations, formal and informal, e.g. classroom routines, peer teaching
- questions to clarify or gain further information
- explains cause and effect, e.g. *She fell off the bar because she was trying a somersault for the first time, then her hand slipped*
- follows instructions that include two or three elements.

Teaching Notes

When children begin school they are challenged to speak and respond in many different contexts, both formal and informal, spontaneous or practised. Their ability to use particular forms of language is influenced greatly by the range and complexity of language experiences provided in the classroom.

Give children opportunities to speak and listen for many *purposes*. Each of these purposes should place different demands on the way language is used. For example:
- to express feelings, ideas and experiences
- to develop a positive attitude to speaking and listening
- to develop proficiency in speaking and listening as a tool for effective communication
- to explore and maintain relationships
- to describe or explain experiences or ideas
- to predict and make comparisons
- to clarify thoughts and express understandings
- to entertain or amuse
- to evaluate

Encourage children to speak and listen with a variety of *audiences* in both formal and informal situations. Providing children with models of language will extend their own understanding and use of language.

Arrange learning experiences that help children see the links between spoken and other forms of language. In this way the development of oral language skills will lead naturally and logically into reading and writing.

Provide activities across the curriculum that incorporate experiences with speaking, listening, reading and writing.

Structure situations that place increasingly complex demands on the way children use language, e.g. giving explanations, retelling a story, interpreting characters, justifying choices.

Introduce and promote content language, i.e. vocabulary and language related to reading, writing, mathematics, science, social studies etc.

Major Teaching Emphases

◆ **provide opportunities to listen and respond to stories, songs and poems**
◆ **develop the language necessary to express an understanding of narrative structure, e.g. giving logical, sequenced retells, describing setting, characters and events, or incorporating literary language**
◆ **assist students to use different styles of language to suit a range of audiences and purposes**

- ◆ **include collaborative and exploratory activities that encourage children to predict, hypothesise and make comparisons** ·
- ◆ **promote language that allows children to discuss and express opinions related to topics, issues and interests**
- ◆ **introduce subject-specific vocabulary through oral, written and reading activities**
- ◆ **develop students' ability to ask and answer questions as a strategy for solving problems**
- ◆ **help students present factual information clearly and logically**
- • encourage students to recount experiences
- • promote speaking and listening skills through play and improvised drama
- • help students to give and receive simple explanations and instructions

At all phases:
- ◆ **provide models of correct English**
- ◆ **ensure that students encounter a range of purposes, audiences and situations that challenge them to use language in many different ways**
- ◆ **allow time to practise the sounds, rhythms, words and structures of language**
- ◆ **make links between oral and written language**
- ◆ **encourage students to respond to a range of oral and visual texts**
- ◆ **value the processes of group interaction.**

◆ *Entries in bold are considered critical to the children's further development*

Establishing an Environment for Speaking and Listening

It is important that teachers establish a learning environment that provides opportunities for children to use language in situations with a purpose and meaning that is obvious to them. Children are more likely to express their ideas and understandings when they are in a caring environment, where others listen and show an interest in and respect for what they have to say. The quality of language produced in the classroom will reflect the way teachers and children interact in one-to-one, group and whole-class situations. Children should be encouraged to talk to teachers, other adults and peers to ask questions, express ideas and opinions, and share information.

Ways to Create an Environment for Speaking and Listening

- Create a classroom that motivates children to interact and use oral language for a variety of purposes with a range of audiences. Include areas for specific activities, materials, children's interests, small groups, large groups.
- Arrange furniture and seating to allow children to explore, create and move around freely.
- Provide a balance between quiet and noisy areas, e.g. a quiet reading corner, activity centres, construction area.
- Include an area for the whole class to gather for sharing ideas, conducting discussions and introducing literature. Display books, calendars, weather charts, an easel for holding big books etc. Consider the ways children can listen to and practise different models of language.
- Provide materials for independent activities that will stimulate conversation and discussion.
- Establish a class library that contains a variety of reading materials, both commercially-produced and class-generated. Encourage children to express opinions about favourite or interesting books.
- Read to children daily. Include texts that have a range of styles and topics. Talk about the print, graphics, authors' style, children's impressions of the texts.
- Teach and recite rhymes, poetry, finger plays.
- Read books that include rhyme, rhythm and repetition.
- Read or tell traditional tales. Encourage children to join in whenever particular words, phrases or sentences are repeated.
- Provide aids to assist children to retell stories. Include felt boards, masks, headbands, cardboard cut-outs, sequence pictures.
- Create stories to accompany textless books, posters or sets of pictures. Discuss and exchange ideas about possible settings, characters and sequences of events.

- Provide masks and have children generate background information about the characters. Create and dramatise the stories.
- Encourage children to play with words. For example, identify words and phrases in literature with onomatopoeic qualities:
  - Action: tick-tock of a clock, trip-trap of hooves, clickety-clack of a train
  - Sound: slither, sizzle, splash, creak, groan, howl
    Include the words in drama, music or movement activities.
- Provide a cassette or listening post with a selection of stories, songs or 'read-along' books.
- Organise storytelling or reading sessions that involve teachers, library staff, parents and older children. Encourage children to participate through drama, music and art or have them retell their own stories.
- Play charades or introduce miming activities. Include nursery rhymes, simple stories, occupations, topic-related situations.
- Play games that require participants to give or receive instructions, e.g. 'Pin the tail on the ...', barrier games, commercial games.
- Provide opportunities to speak and listen as often as possible with a variety of people in a range of situations. Include formal and informal tasks, e.g. conversations with peers, conveying messages, greeting guests.
- Set up a writing corner with a range of pens, pencils, paper, card. Encourage children to interact with their peers through writing and talking about letters, greeting cards, messages etc.
- Plan and talk about writing experiences across the curriculum.
- Create a print-rich environment. Display labels, signs, descriptions and speech balloons on murals, charts, poems, songs, calendars, weather charts, samples of

children's work. Talk about the displays and encourage children to add their own items of interest or topic-related resources. Motivate children to interact with print by challenging them to discover 'something wrong' each day. Introduce 'errors' such as a reversed speech balloon, incorrect names or missing text. Make sure children realise this is a deliberate mistake so that they do not use it as a model.

- Talk with children about their writing. Publish and display class books.
- Continue 'Shared Book Experience' that provides opportunities to demonstrate what fluent reading sounds like and how language works. Such experiences help children learn about phonics, high-frequency words and reading strategies through real reading experiences.
- Talk about authors, titles and illustrations. Have children predict the outcome of a narrative or the content of an informational text.
- Display alphabet friezes, sing alphabet songs, make alphabet books and discuss sound-symbol relationships.
- Encourage children to have-a-go at spelling and praise all attempts.
- Display and talk about words commonly used in children's writing. Encourage children to aim for conventional spelling in high-frequency words.
- Play games that draw children's attention to letters, sounds and patterns in words, e.g. dominoes, word sorts, 'What Comes Next?' (see *Word Study* chapter in *Spelling: Resource Book*).
- Share class news. Model how to reflect on an experience, select the key elements and present information in a logical sequence.
- Encourage spontaneous make-believe and role play. Such experiences provide children with opportunities to talk through new concepts, relive experiences and experiment with new ideas. Provide a selection of non-specific materials to activate children's imagination, e.g. boxes, household implements, dress-up clothes.
- Set up a puppet corner. Include a selection of commercial and class-made puppets. Provide a tray of paper, card, glue, scissors and junk materials. Encourage children to produce their own puppets.
- Provide interest or learning centres to stimulate discussion and literacy-related activities:
  - Home corner. Add calendars, message boards, telephones, telephone books. Supply writing materials and model different purposes for writing, e.g. sending greeting cards, writing shopping lists, composing a letter. Encourage children to produce their own examples of writing during role play activities.
  - Telephone corner. Provide a set of telephones and message pads. Encourage children to make calls and record messages or information. Model language for making or receiving calls, e.g. to a friend, parent, take-away store, ambulance.
  - Shop or shops. Consider a supermarket, card shop, newsagent, greengrocer or restaurant. Provide items such as shopping baskets, cash register, catalogues, newspapers, money, empty food packets, purses, scales. Include paper and pencils for writing shopping lists. Introduce relevant vocabulary and encourage children to incorporate these terms in role-play activities.
  - Restaurant or fast food outlet. Supply aprons, cutlery, chairs, plates, menus, money. Add writing materials for shopping lists, taking orders, making menus and totalling the day's takings. Model appropriate language, vocabulary and behaviours.
  - Post Office. Display and discuss purpose of envelopes, stamps, parcels, scales etc. Provide materials for children to use during role-play activities. If possible, include a postbox and encourage children to write to friends, other classes, teachers or community members. Allocate children to sort and deliver mail each day.
  - Hospital, doctor's or dentist's surgery. Provide materials that can be reorganised to suit the particular role play. Include writing materials for prescriptions or appointment books.
- Integrate drama activities in music, storytelling and curriculum-related topics. Model how language and vocabulary can express feelings, communicate ideas, recall experiences or narrate stories. Involve children in designing and producing props and puppets for dramatic activities.
- Introduce a variety of music-related activities such as singing, chanting, experimenting with instruments, listening and moving to music.
- Include outdoor areas as part of the learning environment, e.g. use climbing equipment as props when dramatising traditional stories.

Speech Development

(See p. 51)
Children develop clear speech by communicating with others. The more exposure they have to correct forms, the faster they will move towards adult patterns of language. If children are still overgeneralising at this stage, model adult forms of speech and provide opportunities to practise and refine their English language use. In addition, provide access to a variety of speech models so that children appreciate the importance of effective communication, e.g. clear pronunciation, appropriate volume, logical ordering of ideas, relevant detail, etc.

Initially, respond to the meaning of the children's message rather than its form. Clarify unclear communication through questioning, paraphrasing or commenting.

- Introduce appropriate language forms incidentally or incorporate specific language patterns during discussion, poetry, drama, shared reading, role play etc.
- Encourage spontaneous conversation and discussion.
- Model standard speech and language forms in context.
- Identify, discuss and role play situations that require the use of standard English:
  – introducing visitors
  – conveying a message
  – speaking at assembly
  – seeking information.
- Avoid interrupting unnecessarily as it may interfere with children's train of thought.
- Try to avoid predicting what children are going to say and doing the talking for them.
- When children consistently use incorrect forms of speech, introduce alternatives incidentally without forcing attention away from the meaning of what is being said:
  Child: *We seen a shark on the weekend.*
  Teacher: *Yes, some other children saw one at the same beach.*
- Share the language of others by listening to stories being told or read by other children, teachers, visitors etc. Discuss positively how pronunciation, pace, volume etc. influence the effectiveness of the message.
- Include activities in which the children focus on particular language structures, e.g. choral speaking, singing, assembly items. Provide time to practise and reflect on features of effective communication, e.g. clear pronunciation, appropriate volume, non-verbal gestures such as looking at the audience, standing correctly.

- Provide opportunities for formal and informal talk:
  – conversing with peers, teachers and other adults during classroom activities
  – discussing, collaborating during group work
  – introducing and thanking visitors
  – making tape recordings
  – listening to, and evaluating, cassettes
  – telephoning to convey or request information.
- Introduce songs and rhymes that feature repetitive language. Use percussion instruments or clapping to highlight rhythms and sounds.
- Have children record instructions for others to follow. Discuss the importance of clear speech and explicit instructions. Include instructions to:
  – make a model
  – complete a reading activity
  – solve a mathematical problem
  – locate information to complete a puzzle, e.g. find treasure on a map.
- Draw children's attention to the differences between speaking and writing:
  – compare the way language is used to convey the same content in a phone message and a letter
  – discuss alternative ways of using language to communicate the message more effectively, e.g. *What's a different way of saying/writing it? Who can think of a better word?*
  – demonstrate how meaning is made explicit in spoken and written texts, i.e. spoken texts rely on stress, intonation, volume, gesture; written texts rely on punctuation.

Language of Social Interaction

(See p. 51)

Language plays an important role in the personal and social development of children. It helps them to explore, establish and maintain relationships. It also enables them to share ideas, solve problems together, exchange experiences and show consideration and respect for others.

Social skills develop as children learn to communicate appropriately and efficiently. In the classroom, teachers can provide children with many opportunities to use different styles of language in different situations. All children need to practise and adapt language to suit particular audiences, both formal and informal. They also need to be exposed to appropriate models of courtesy, respect and polite behaviour. Children will be more inclined to adopt these behaviours if they are seen as an established feature of classroom routines.

The *Oral Language: Resource Book* chapter *Language of Social Interaction* outlines strategies that assist children to adapt language for many situations and purposes. The nature of the audience influences the type of speaking and listening that occurs in the classroom. Possible audiences include child to child, child to group, child to teacher, child to other adults.

- Peers. Provide opportunities for children to interact with their peers, both inside and outside the classroom, e.g. working in groups, partner activities, peer tutoring.

Include activities in which children also interact with younger and older peers.
- Child to teacher. Encourage children to discuss, question and reflect on what they are doing. Provide a range of language models, e.g. conversing, explaining, instructing, describing, questioning. Observe and monitor the different ways children use language and help them to be more aware of appropriate language styles in different situations.
- Child to adults. Provide children with opportunities to interact with many adults, e.g. other teachers, support staff, visitors. Involve parents and other adults in school activities:
  - solve problems during activity maths
  - plan actions before an excursion
  - create characters and scenarios during reading.

- Conversation. Introduce topics and resources that motivate children to engage in spontaneous conversation, e.g. through a display, introduction of new resources, an unexpected visitor or event. Stimulate more purposeful or directed conversation by introducing topics, outlining problems, raising issues, showing charts etc. Use the experiences to model and discuss appropriate social behaviours, e.g. listening to others, reacting courteously, inquiring, thanking or interrupting in an appropriate manner.
Role play conversations related to appropriate and inappropriate behaviour:
  - general good manners, e.g. *thank you, please*
  - offering help and taking turns
  - greetings; daily greetings, friends, special occasions
  - listening politely and asking for permission
  - introducing visitors
  - inviting friends and accepting invitations.
Use puppets to model conversation. Have children role play courteous behaviours with their peers.

- Discussion. Organise whole-class and small-group discussions in a range of subject areas. Through discussion, children develop social skills and learn content and vocabulary more thoroughly. Organisational formats may include:
  - all groups discussing one topic
  - all groups discussing a different topic
  - the class discussing different aspects of a topic
  - whole-class discussion preceding small-group discussion.

Choose topics related to the children's experiences:
- home, family, pets, games, literature
- hobbies
- classroom activities.

If children need guidance to develop discussion skills, provide a model for them to follow. Young children, in particular, will need an adult to initiate the discussion and encourage all to participate. Demonstrate appropriate polite behaviour and provide examples of comments or questions needed to gain or clarify information.

- Discuss concerns and ways to resolve them. Introduce role plays that help children develop an awareness of the ideas or opinions of others:
  - different interpretations of a classroom or schoolyard incident
  - reaching consensus on a group task
  - justifying the choice of a classroom activity
  - dealing with loss or damage to personal property.

  Provide children with opportunities to talk about feelings related to themselves, other people, classroom organisation, activities etc. In groups, list and discuss things that make them feel happy, sad, excited, frightened, proud etc. Have groups compare lists, identifying similarities and differences.

  Introduce strategies for developing effective group discussion:
  - participants' responsibilities
  - waiting quietly for turn
  - speaking clearly
  - listening politely
  - helping group reach final consensus or opinion.

- Brainstorming. Brainstorm ideas related to classroom interests or topics. Accept all ideas then classify them:
  - important/not important
  - need more discussion.

  Talk about the social skills involved in respecting others' ideas, opinions and feelings.

- Explanations. Include and model explanations in all subject areas. Introduce relevant vocabulary and encourage children to question their peers to elicit or clarify information, e.g. *What is it? How did you make it? Did you have any problems?* Depending on the situation and purpose, children use language to describe, direct, inform, predict, justify or evaluate. Emphasise the importance of responding to the needs of the audience to ensure that the explanation is logical and clearly understood:
  - give instructions for others to complete a task
  - explain how to play a game
  - explain how to reproduce a pattern in maths
  - give directions for locating resources in the library
  - explain how to follow a recipe.

- Messages. Give children responsibility for relaying or conveying information. Such experiences develop careful listening and thinking, and clear speaking.

Involve other children, teachers, support staff, parents, visitors. Help children to listen for information, seek clarification if necessary and speak clearly when delivering the message.

- Telephoning. Provide a set of telephones and model correct procedures for making or receiving calls. Encourage children to use the telephones during role-play activities.

- Guidelines for classroom behaviour. Observe and monitor children's behaviour in various situations, e.g. group discussions, playground activities, partner work. Reflect on and discuss observations with the children. Work together to devise classroom rules related to courteous speaking and listening. Record rules on charts.

- Excursions and visits. Include direct experiences to broaden children's general knowledge and expose them to a range of language styles. Visit people in the immediate school environment, e.g. library, dental clinic, canteen or administration block. In addition, visit areas of interest in the local neighbourhood, e.g. shopping centre, post office, veterinary clinic, retirement village, community library. Children should also have opportunities to plan and participate in excursions in the wider community, e.g. theatre, zoo, museum, art gallery, neighbouring town.

- Speaking and listening corner. Establish a speaking and listening corner that motivates children to engage in conversations, discussions, storytelling, explanations, descriptions or information hunts. Stimulus material might include:
  - cassette players and tapes
  - art and crafts materials
  - books
  - pictures, charts, photographs.

- Guest speakers. Invite guest speakers to talk about interests, occupations or community issues. Before the visit, discuss appropriate speaking and listening behaviours:
  - meeting the visitor
  - introducing the visitor and topic
  - listening attentively
  - asking relevant questions
  - expressing thanks.

Language and Literacy

(See p. 51)

At this stage, children need to see the links between spoken and other forms of language. They need to realise that written language functions in a similar way to oral and aural language—that both provide a means of communicating ideas and information. Children's understandings about reading and writing evolve from their proficiency as speakers and listeners. To achieve success in literacy, children need many opportunities to write and talk about their writing; to read and listen to others read; and to engage in purposeful activities in which speaking, listening, reading and writing are interrelated.

They also need to know that oral and written language are often different.

The *Oral Language: Resource Book* chapter *Language and Literacy* outlines strategies and activities for developing literacy understandings through oral language.

- Newstelling. Newstelling requires children to recall, sequence and summarise experiences or events for presentation to an audience. Assist children to select and organise information by providing a 'news' chart that includes the elements of a recount—*when, who, where, what*. Model how to link information to each element and encourage children to use the chart when planning their own news item. (See *Newstelling* section of *Literacy-related Skills* Module.)

- Linking newstelling into writing. Discuss how the elements of a recount are the same for an oral or written presentation—*when, who, where, what*. Model how to generate a news plan by drawing pictures or writing notes under key words. Brainstorm as much specific information as possible. Use the plan to write an extended recount.
- Oral sharing activities. Encourage children to report on experiences related to classroom activities, e.g. cooking, art and crafts activities, mathematics tasks:
  - move into groups to tell news
  - have one child from each group tell news to the class
  - use a microphone, TV set or puppets for variation
  - discuss content, vocabulary, responses to audience, questions asked.

- News pictures. Have children draw or paint their news. Use the resource as an aid for planning and presenting the recount. Encourage the audience to question for further information or clarification.

- 'Show and Tell' news. Model how to describe the attributes or functions of an item. Display a description chart and add or delete attribute headings as the children develop proficiency in using descriptive language.
- Topic news. Assist children to prepare and present reports based on personal experiences or interests, e.g. my pet, hobbies, favourite books.
- Sharing across the curriculum. Prepare and present oral reports on curriculum-related topics, e.g. social studies, mathematics, science. Provide frameworks to assist planning:
  - describing the task
  - explaining how the task was completed
  - reflecting on process and product.
- Presenting to different audiences. Present news items or oral reports to different classes, assembly audiences, unseen audiences (through video or audio tapes).

- News tape exchange. Prepare news tapes to exchange with other classes. Discuss the type of audience and need to make information more explicit. Include:
  - news items
  - reports and other information
  - stories, poems, songs etc.
- Sharing knowledge. Report to others after curriculum-related research. Research may involve books, magazines, newspapers, television, drawing, noting ideas, talking with others. Provide a framework to assist children in planning and presenting the report:
  - What is the topic?
  - Where did you find information?
  - What did you discover?

- Describing characters. Select characters from a story being read or told. Brainstorm physical features and personal attributes. Work in groups to prepare and present individual profiles.
- Modelling stories. Model the language and structure of stories for children who have had limited exposure to print. Use play materials such as small dolls, furniture, animals, cars etc. Create a spontaneous story for children, focusing on both the storyline and appropriate language. Encourage the children to add to or retell the story. Make the props available during free activities so children are motivated to create their own stories.
- Creating stories from pictures. With the class, create an oral story to accompany a textless book, set of pictures or cartoon without words, or a poster. Discuss the importance of:
  - the setting
  - the characters
  - the sequence of events.

- Interviewing characters. Conduct shared-book sessions with a traditional story. When children are familiar with the story-line, display one page of the book and discuss the characters and events. Choose children to role play the scene and ask the audience to devise questions relating to the characters' intentions, motivations, problems, relationship with other characters etc.
- Creating stories from character masks. Display masks and work together to brainstorm possible backgrounds for the characters, e.g. *She's a dentist. She might be a friend. I think it's his dog.* Suggest actions that could form the basis for a story and have children role play the scenario. Encourage the audience to suggest further actions or dialogue. When children are familiar with the procedure, have small groups create and present their stories to the class.
- Changing the ending. Read or tell a story, omitting the ending. Have the children draw, write or suggest possible conclusions. Compare ideas and select the most appropriate choice. Alternatively, combine several ideas or role play all suggestions.
- Telling stories in sequence. Prepare sets of pictures relating to a familiar story. Have children work in groups to sequence the pictures and prepare a retell for the class. When children are familiar with the activity, make the task more challenging by providing sets of pictures relating to an unfamiliar story or sequence of events.

- Circle stories. Conduct a shared-book session with a traditional story. Discuss the setting, characters, problems, events and conclusion. Model how to create a progressive story by taking turns to add to and develop the previous speaker's contribution. Make the activity more challenging by providing 'story starters' such as pictures, props, character profiles or settings. The children must use their imagination to develop an entertaining and logical storyline.
- Talking about books. Encourage children to tell friends, children in other classes, teachers, parents etc. about a book that has been read recently and enjoyed. Provide pictures, paintings, puppets etc. to assist in describing the story. Focus on talking about, rather than reading, the book.

- Telling stories. Organise storytelling sessions that involve teachers, support staff, older children, parents. Encourage children to participate in the sessions through choral speaking, drama, art, music. Motivate children to tell their own stories.
- Shared reading. Conduct shared reading sessions. Encourage children to join in with, and discuss, the text. Explain how stories can be told in an oral or written form.
- Predicting and justifying story-lines. Look at the title and illustrations of a story, poem or play. Discuss possible developments and conclusions. Encourage children to justify their decisions by relating to the illustrations. Read the story and compare children's predictions.
- Identifying cause and effect in stories. Read or tell stories and identify how each event influences the characters' actions or reactions.
- Informal texts. Discuss how these texts show different ways of interpreting and presenting information. When introducing titles:
  - encourage children to contribute their own experiences to the topic
  - provide opportunities to contribute ideas and listen to the ideas of others
  - motivate children to talk about, or report on, the topic in pairs or small groups
  - discuss how information can be presented through words, photographs, illustrations, headings, tables.

- Developing vocabulary. Help children to extend the range of words used and understood, and to incorporate more specialised vocabulary, where appropriate.
- Brainstorming. Brainstorm ideas orally or in written form. Choose topics related to literature, social studies, excursions:
  - brainstorm character attributes
  - brainstorm observations after an excursion
  - brainstorm possible questions for an interview.
- Use terminology. Introduce and provide practice in using correct subject-specific vocabulary:
  - mathematical terms
  - reading vocabulary
  - science terminology.

- Modelling descriptive vocabulary. Model how to describe events, people, objects, feelings etc. Develop an awareness that the language of description enables people to report experiences or objects in a more comprehensive way. Provide opportunities for children to use descriptive language in oral and written activities:
  - describe story characters
  - describe science experiments
  - play barrier games
  - complete classification activities
  - play 'What am I?' games.

- Modelled writing. Conduct oral sharing sessions that assist children to make the links between oral and written forms:
  - explain how thoughts are organised, decisions made, words and sentences produced
  - model and discuss various forms of writing, e.g. narrative, poetry, lists, speech balloons, reports, recounts.
- Linking oral and written narratives to writing. Write letters to characters, authors, illustrators, Discuss the draft with a peer or teacher. Read the published copy to the class.
- Writing instructions. Play barrier games and write a set of instructions for others to read and follow. (Refer First Steps *Oral Language: Resource Book*.)
- Cooperative stories. Create oral stories in groups, and record final version in print.

Language and Thinking

(See p. 51)

Children at this stage use language to express, reshape and clarify their thoughts in both informal and more structured situations. Teachers should continue to provide children with opportunities to use language to formulate ideas and concepts, to question, demonstrate understandings and share discoveries with adults and peers.

The *Oral Language: Resource Book* chapter *Language and Thinking* outlines strategies and activities for developing cognitive skills.

- Demonstrating knowledge. An effective method for demonstrating knowledge of a topic is to tell someone else about it—peers, teachers or other adults. Organise lessons to include sharing times, either during or after the activity. This approach motivates children to monitor what they are doing, reflect on the activity and select information for the listener. Initially, provide support by modelling how to plan and present information:
  – include the purpose for sharing
  – describe what has been produced
  – explain how it was produced
  – provide an evaluative comment.
- Working in groups. Problems are easier to solve when children can share their thoughts and ideas with others. Organise a range of partner or group activities that challenge children to cooperate, share ideas, listen and respond to others' contributions. When children work interactively they can refine their thinking skills, demonstrate and explain processes to others, or explore possibilities through discussion, questioning and observation:
  – solve mathematical problems together
  – explore and explain possibilities during science experiments
  – work together on a reading task
  – write a short play together
  – plan a puppet day
  – practise and present a cumulative story.

- Problem solving. Children develop thinking skills when they use language to experiment, explore and solve problems. Take time to create open-ended tasks that have a range of solutions and a variety of approaches for tackling them. Focus on the process and thinking involved in the tasks rather than the product. Encourage children to explore, experiment, observe, discuss, and express their understandings to peers and adults:
  – complete jigsaws and other puzzles
  – draw a procedure from written instructions
  – write a procedure from illustrations
  – invent a simple machine and explain its function and operation
  – discover a location from written instructions
  – find treasure on a treasure map.
- Developing curiosity. Motivate children to show curiosity about the natural and physical environment:
  – observe, compare and talk about plant growth
  – manipulate and discuss construction materials
  – work with a partner to compare estimates of length, weight, height, size, number
  – categorise and compare animals
  – speculate on the outcome of problem-solving activities
  – predict the outcome of experiments
  – brainstorm possible alternatives for finding solutions
  – compare different groups' outcomes and processes for solving problems.
- Finding solutions. Introduce some activities with a question, e.g. *Which shapes can tessellate? What is the best design for a kite?* Motivate the children to work together to experiment and find solutions. Provide a range of books, charts and open-ended materials. Conclude with a sharing time in which children can reflect on the process, product, difficulties and successes of the activity.
- Mathematics. Introduce mathematical activities that develop concepts and vocabulary in meaningful situations. Encourage children to predict outcomes of activities and link previous experiences to new situations:
  – include movement activities to develop concepts of space
  – work with a partner to identify and discuss shapes in the environment
  – make a group collage of photographs that display pattern and symmetry

- construct 2-D and 3-D models of the school, local shopping centre or surrounding streets
- organise group construction activities that must be a certain height, cover a specified area, include a nominated number of blocks
- sort, classify and make sets of objects using own criteria
- sort objects and describe features such as *bigger than, smaller than, wider.*
- Classification. Assist children to develop thinking skills by classifying what they observe, know, read or discuss:
  - provide topic-related pictures or items and have children sort them according to their own rules. Have other children guess the rules
  - provide the criteria for sorting, e.g. living and non-living
  - work with a partner to sort pictures or information for a graph
  - classify pictures or information on semantic grids
  - classify storybook characters according to their personalities, actions, motives.
- Planning. Involve children in planning and organising classroom activities, excursions or school camps. Encourage children to relate the discussions to past experiences, to predict what they might see or do, to help plan the activities, and to compare their expectations with what occurs.

SCHOOL CAMP
– SORRENTO
Can you guess what we might see?

- a dolphin
- sharks
- fishing boats
- a marina
- an oil tanker
- tourists
- shells
- sand erosion
- bushland
- kangaroos
- rabbits
- wildflowers
- bush tracks

- Asking questions. Model how to ask questions to clarify and gain information or analyse and explore ideas. Teach children the question words—*when, who, where, what, why*—that elicit different types of information. Introduce activities that motivate children to practise questioning skills:
  - conduct interviews with school or community people
  - introduce open-ended tasks that have a range of solutions
  - provide a variety of materials for solving problems
  - interview storybook characters
  - play barrier games.
  Wait for children to question rather than providing them with immediate information.
- Responding to questions. Avoid asking questions that elicit only closed responses. Questions should be

sufficiently challenging to raise the level of children's thinking:
  - ask questions that require children to clarify their ideas, e.g. during problem-solving activities
  - ask questions to stimulate and extend thinking, e.g. during science experiments
  - help children reflect on their thinking, e.g. explaining how they completed a puzzle
  - ask questions to help children apply their new knowledge to new situations and present it in different ways, e.g. ask children how they would adapt a completed activity if they were asked to repeat the process.
- Literature. Read a variety of literature and ask questions that motivate children to think about the text:
  - detail—*what, who, when …?*
  - sequence—*What happened after …?*
  - comparisons—*How were they alike/different?*
  - cause and effect—*Why did …?*
  - character traits—*Which part describes …?*
- Expressing feelings. Provide children with opportunities to express their feelings:
  - respond to music and literature
  - talk about things that make them sad, happy, excited
  - express opinions about people, books, experiences
  - display books, photographs, charts that show different emotions or evoke emotional responses.
- Imaginative play. Allow children time to develop feelings, ideas and understandings through drama, role play and fantasy. Encourage them to engage in spontaneous and directed activities related to literature, music, social studies, real and imagined events.
- Listening. Provide children with opportunities to listen for a variety of purposes. When children have something to listen *for*, rather than listen *to*, more effective learning takes place:
  - ask questions before a story to provide a focus for listening
  - encourage children to develop reading comprehension skills by focusing on the main idea and support information
  - promote critical listening by inviting children to evaluate what they have heard
  - listen to and carry out a series of verbal instructions
  - listen, then question to clarify or obtain additional information.

For Parents

How can I help my child with speaking and listening?

- Set aside 10-15 minutes to discuss what has happened during the day.
- Involve your child in conversations, plans and discussions.
- Ask and answer questions.
- Involve your child in adult conversations, when appropriate.
- Encourage your child to give reasons for decisions he or she has made, and use logical arguments when trying to present points of view.
- Listen carefully and clarify meaning by paraphrasing your child's contributions.
- Provide a good listening model and avoid responding with 'Mmm' or 'Just a minute'.
- Talk about topics of mutual interest with the expectation that your child will listen.
- Encourage your child to share and talk about experiences with a range of people, e.g. peers, relations, other adults.
- Teach your child to use the telephone.
- Read to your child and talk about the print and illustrations.

- Help your child to read books brought from school, e.g. talk about the title, illustrations and content.
- Ask your child to retell a story or explain a favourite section.
- Point out similarities in the way words look or sound.
- Read school newsletters together.
- Take an interest in writing produced at school.
- Talk about the purposes for writing, e.g. to make a shopping list, send a birthday card, write a letter. Show different ways of writing and provide paper and pencils for your child to have-a-go.
- Talk about the variety of print forms in magazines, newspapers, telephone books, comics.
- Focus on the message children assign to their writing rather than correct letter formations or spelling.
- Play language games, e.g. *I Spy*, rhyming words, locating signs along the road, telling jokes and riddles.
- Play games such as *Scrabble, Chinese Checkers, Snakes and Ladders*.
- Watch and discuss television programs or videos.
- Include mealtimes as talking times. Encourage all family members to participate.
- Join a book library and toy library.

PHASE 5 Consolidated Language for Learning

In this phase, children use a variety of language forms and manipulate language to suit a range of situations. They also understand how listening, speaking, reading and writing complement each other as tools for learning.

Example of newstelling: Gerard (Year 4)

… Good morning, girls and boys. On the weekend we went to Burns Beach. When we got onto the sand my Dad found a raft and he pulled it out into the water … um, I think it was pretty old because it was starting to rot, so we dragged it into the water to see if it would sink … don't know how it got in the sand … don't think it floated in … probably someone brought it there … anyway, it, um, floated a bit and floated near the rocks and got stuck, so we went for a walk and Dad nearly stepped on a death adder.

Audience: *What's a death raider?*

… Death adders. They're snakes, little snakes with a grey colour and they're poisonous … You'd need help if you got bitten … have to leave in a hurry.

Example of explanation after group activity:

… Well, we used this stuff, wire, to make it stand up. John covered the dinosaur shape with lots of strips of paper in glue. You had to let it dry and it was gooey for a while … we could have used more papier mâché but we didn't have time … so we decided to push the shape around a bit … I mixed the paint and we both painted it … it ran a bit here but it still looks OK … We'll stick some marbles for eyes … Oh, yeah, John thinks we should have some scary music playing near it.

Assessing Gerard's Oral Language

- adapts language to meet social and situational needs
- increasingly using intonation, facial expressions and gestures as tools for communicating ideas and feelings
- ◆ **communicates effectively by sharing ideas, offering advice, opinion and information**
- ◆ **demonstrates the ability to develop a topic in curriculum-related situations, e.g. reporting, describing, comparing**
- adds evaluative comments to enhance spoken presentations
- ◆ **uses appropriately specialised vocabulary in a variety of situations**
- ◆ **continues to develop reason and logic, using more refined language**
- explains cause and effect relationships

The teacher's observations during these and other classroom activities indicate that Gerard is in the *Consolidated Language for Learning* phase.

Consolidated Language for Learning Indicators

Language of Social Interaction
(See p. 70)

The speaker/listener:

◆ **communicates effectively by sharing ideas, offering advice, opinion and information and reacting to the contributions of others**

- shows an increasing awareness of social conventions, e.g. *Could you tell me where...? Mrs Carroll asked if you would...*
- reacts according to own perceptions in a conflict situation, but is able to appreciate another's point of view through adult mediation
- adapts language to meet different social and situational needs, talking to friends at netball is different from meeting friends of parents
- monitors others' speech and paraphrases content, e.g. *I felt really angry when the group wouldn't co-operate*
- uses intonation, facial expressions and gestures as tools for communicating ideas and feelings
- uses jargon or slang with peers.

Language and Literacy
(See p. 72)

The speaker/listener:

◆ **recognises that language is adapted to meet different social, situational and educational needs, e.g. the language of reporting is different from the language of interviewing or story-telling**

◆ **demonstrates the ability to develop a topic in curriculum-related situations, e.g. reporting, describing, comparing**

◆ **interprets texts from own point of view— expresses opinions, draws conclusions**

◆ **uses appropriately specialised vocabulary and structures in a variety of situations, e.g. discussions, reports, modified debates**

- shows evidence of planning during recounts
- adds appropriate elaboration and detail to recounts and describes events, objects and concepts outside immediate experience, e.g. community news
- adds evaluative comments to enhance spoken presentations, e.g. *I believe that recycling is very important and we all need to take it a lot more seriously*
- demonstrates knowledge of difference between narrative and informational texts
- incorporates literary expressions when describing or discussing narrative texts, e.g. repetition of the phrase made the story flow

- is able to describe the setting, events and characters of stories/films/television dramas succinctly
- retells stories of some complexity, individually or in groups
- makes comparisons between narrative and informational texts
- uses similes and metaphors to enhance meaning
- shows knowledge of language structure, e.g. uses conjunctions effectively to express relationships between ideas; maintains and manipulates tones and mood appropriately; provides referents when using pronouns
- discusses rules of language, grammar
- recognises subtle differences in words, e.g. shimmery/ shiny, cross/angry, eat/devour
- is able to describe the significant content of stories, television dramas and films succinctly.

Language and Thinking
(See p. 75)

The speaker/listener:

◆ **continues to develop reason and logic, by attempting to draw conclusions, make inferences, justify and explain statements; asking questions and seeking confirmation**

◆ **listens to evaluate, draw inferences and make judgements**

- investigates problems and sees a range of solutions
- offers definitions of words, usually by functions
- considers possible cause/effect relationships and justifies the most appropriate, e.g. *At first I thought it was the slope that increased the car speed but it could also be the smooth surface of the track*
- follows complex sequences of instructions
- evaluates the consistency of information across several sentences
- initiates questions to gain clarification or further information
- uses language for puns, jokes, riddles and sarcasm.

Teaching Notes

In this phase, students extend their use of language as both speakers and listeners. They use a wide variety of language forms and can manipulate language to suit a range of purposes and situations.

Students are developing an understanding of how speaking, listening, writing and reading complement each other as tools for communication and that these forms of language are common to all curriculum areas. For example, they use language to explain mathematical problems, report on science experiments, or compare narrative and informational texts.

Help students develop *proficiency* in speaking and listening so they can communicate effectively and efficiently. They need to articulate their ideas in a logical, fluent manner that is readily understood by the listener. They also need to extend the range of words understood and used, and to develop specialised *vocabulary* linked to curriculum topics.

Continue to encourage students to use appropriate methods of communication in a variety of situations and for a variety of purposes. For example:

- to express feelings, observations, ideas during group discussion
- to relate experiences to peers
- to entertain visitors through puppetry
- to explore and maintain relationships through role play
- to seek information through community interviews
- to give information through an assembly report
- to direct others by devising rules for a game
- to make comparisons of story characters
- to predict, speculate and hypothesise during cooperative maths activities.

Major Teaching Emphases

- ◆ **help students to present factual information in a clear and logical way**
- ◆ **help students to discuss increasingly complex issues taking others' views into consideration**
- ◆ **help students to assess and interpret arguments and opinions**
- ◆ **implement activities that require students to present ideas, experiences and understandings in all curriculum areas**
- ◆ **help students to use specialised vocabulary**
- ◆ **include small-group and whole-group activities that focus on joint sharing, problem-solving, negotiation and consensus**
- ◆ **help students to talk to and respond to wider audiences using a variety of language styles**
- ◆ **help students to summarise main ideas**
- ◆ **help students to express and justify own opinions**
- • provide students with opportunities to recount events and narrate stories

- provide opportunities to extend the range of words used and understood
- help students to ask increasingly precise or detailed questions, and respond to increasingly complex instructions and questions

At all phases:
- **provide models of correct English**
- **ensure that students encounter a range of purposes, audiences and situations that challenge them to use language in many different ways**
- **allow time to practise the sounds, rhythms, words and structures of language**
- **make links between oral and written language**
- **encourage students to respond to a range of oral and visual texts**
- **value the processes of group interaction.**

- *Entries in bold are considered critical to the children's further development*

Establishing an Environment for Speaking and Listening

Speaking and listening are part of the whole learning process and cannot be developed in isolation. Oral language should provide a background and springboard for developing all language skills across the curriculum. Children should have opportunities to express their opinions, ideas and feelings in an environment that respects the needs, opinions, ideas and feelings of all participants. They should be exposed to purposeful, real-life situations that place increasingly complex demands on the way language is presented and used. Children should have opportunities to modify and extend their ideas through experience, and interaction with others in one-to-one, small-group and whole-class settings. In every situation, children should see oral language as an integral and important part of learning in all curriculum areas.

Ways to Create an Environment for Speaking and Listening

- Create a classroom environment that encourages oral language development. Organise situations and activities in which children can:
    - work with other children to discuss, listen to and exchange ideas
    - develop speaking and listening skills
    - have direct experiences
    - learn from others who have had different experiences
    - find answers to their own questions
    - talk about how they learn.

- Create a classroom that motivates children to speak and interact with a range of teachers, other adults and peers.

- Encourage children to use language for learning in all curriculum areas.

- Encourage children to take more responsibility for their own learning by interacting in both child-initiated activities and teacher-directed tasks.

- Include an area for the whole class to gather for sharing ideas, conducting discussions and introducing literature. Display books, charts, calendars, weather charts, an easel for holding big books, etc.

- Talk about the importance of reading for different purposes, e.g. to gain information, compare information, solve problems, analyse a character's behaviour, enjoy a narrative.

- Continue shared book activities and involve children in discussion of content, style, presentation and conventions. Encourage children to make evaluative comments about the authors' style, illustrations or choice of topics.

- Engage children in oral retells of familiar and unfamiliar narratives.

- Introduce picture storytelling using sequence pictures, single pictures, photographs, topic-related pictures. Encourage children to incorporate descriptive details of characters or events.

- Have a collection of poetry in the classroom. Read and recite poems that motivate children to enjoy the sounds and rhythms of the English language. Choose poems to complement classroom themes, to provide an insight into different poetic style or to reflect cultural backgrounds.

- Introduce choral speaking to re-create the mood and meaning of different poems.

- Introduce puppetry as a strategy for interpreting literature, e.g. work in groups to write a script for a traditional tale. Make puppets and props. Present the puppet play to the class.

- Include drama activities that allow children to express their ideas and listen to the ideas of others.

- Establish learning centres that activate children's thinking and motivate them to share their discoveries with others.

- Work with children to provide a print-rich environment that reflects the interests of the class. Talk about and display subject-specific vocabulary. Encourage an interest in words through crosswords, rhebus activities, word sleuths or other word study activities.

- Provide a selection of commercial and class-made word games. Supply dictionaries and other resources to develop and extend word knowledge.

Language of Social Interaction

(See p. 66)

Language plays an important role in the personal and social development of children. It provides a tool for interaction; the means by which children initiate, explore and maintain relationships with others. Successful social skills emerge as children develop the ability to communicate more effectively and appropriately. Teachers need to help children gain an understanding of themselves and others by providing opportunities to use language to explore and share feelings, values, beliefs and attitudes.

The *Oral Language: Resource Book* chapter *Language of Social Interaction* outlines strategies and activities that assist children to adapt language for many situations and purposes.

The following activites and groupings will assist children's development of appropriate and effective communication skills.

- Peers. Provide opportunities for children to express their opinions and to listen and respond to peers, e.g. working in groups, peer tutoring, discussions, manipulative activities. Plan some situations so that children are also interacting with older and younger children. Interaction with unfamiliar audiences places demands on children to provide more detailed or explicit information.
- Child to teacher. Through experience, children develop their ability to adapt language styles to suit particular audiences and situations. Teachers can promote appropriate language styles by facilitating rather than monopolising talk in the classroom:
  - encourage children to talk to, and with, teachers
  - motivate children to ask questions, speculate and hypothesise
  - provide children with opportunities to express their ideas, understandings and feelings.
- Child to adults. Provide children with opportunities to interact with many adults, e.g. other teachers, adults, parents, community members:
  - share routine daily activities
  - plan school camps or excursions
  - share canteen duties
  - celebrate special days
  - organise art and crafts activities
  - timetable elective programs.
- Small groups. Group size influences the type of interaction in the classroom. To ensure maximum benefit from groups, introduce activities that challenge children to extend language use beyond informal chatter.
- Problem solving. Have the children work in groups to solve a problem by consensus. The problem may be solved in a number of ways, e.g. brainstorming good and bad aspects of possible solutions, suggesting consequences. Explore, discuss and present ideas to others.
- Sharing information. Provide each child with part of the information to complete a task. Children take turns to share their information then work together to complete the activity:
  - reconstruct a poem or story from sections of text
  - play a game
  - complete a puzzle.
- Ranking. Consider priorities for given information. Discuss and complete final ranking through discussion and group consensus:
  - provide photographs of animals and rank those that have adapted most successfully to their environment
  - study occupations and rank those that will be most useful for future generations
  - discuss house designs and rank those that are best suited to hot climates.
- Brainstorming. Organise small groups to share ideas about a topic. Clearly define the type of information to be generated, e.g. food, habitat, location, appearance. Ask groups to summarise and present information to the class.
- Envoy. Introduce and discuss a topic in small groups. After a set time, send an envoy from each group to other groups with the purpose of sharing or collecting further information. When the envoy returns to the 'home' group, information is reported and discussed. Envoying is a useful strategy for teaching discussion skills, developing content knowledge and summarising different points of view.

- Jigsaws. Introduce and discuss a curriculum-related topic. Organise 'home' groups and assign a different number to each child in a group: 1, 2, 3, … All children with identical numbers form 'expert' groups which must concentrate on a specific aspect of a topic, e.g. wind power, water power, nuclear power. The final stage is for participants to return to their 'home' group and report on information obtained from the 'experts'. This information can be used as a springboard for further activities.

- Pair to four. The activity is useful for sharing knowledge and developing discussion skills. Organise partners and assign a task, e.g. share what is known or has been learned about a topic. Set a time limit and stress the importance of each person having an opportunity to share information. At the end of the allocated time, ask each pair to join with another pair. In this grouping, each child reports information obtained from the partner. This approach motivates children to listen carefully, question to clarify information, summarise the partner's understandings and present the key elements to another group.

- Discussion. Organise whole-class and small-group discussions in a range of subject areas. Through discussion, children develop social skills and learn content and vocabulary more thoroughly. Include:
  - all groups discussing one topic
  - all groups discussing a different topic
  - the class discussing different aspects of a topic
  - whole-class discussion preceding small-group discussion.

  Introduce topics that encourage children to reach a deeper understanding of issues through argument, debate or conversation. Children should understand that the outcome of a discussion is not necessarily one correct answer, but rather an exchange of ideas and opinions as issues are explored. Discuss how language is used to influence people.

- Panel discussions. Introduce familiar topics that invite discussion and expression of different opinions, e.g. clearing forests, wearing bike helmets, favourite television programs. Organise a panel comprising several speakers and a chairperson, who invites questions from the audience and allocates them to particular speakers.

- Informal debates. These can be organised along the lines of an open discussion in which all children are encouraged to present and justify their opinions and support or oppose the views of others. Link debates to curriculum topics so children have a broad background knowledge of the content and vocabulary.

- Conversation. Introduce topics, resources and displays that motivate children to engage in spontaneous and directed conversation. In the classroom, purposeful conversation is ensured when topics are of genuine interest and within the realms of the children's experience. Include current events, issues, problems or concerns. Discuss appropriate social courtesies necessary in conversation, e.g. listening carefully, acknowledging different opinions, responding courteously.
  Role play conversations related to appropriate and inappropriate behaviour:
  - general good manners, e.g. *thank you, please*
  - taking turns, offering help
  - asking for permission
  - explaining or offering an apology
  - introducing visitors, greetings when talking with people of different status.

- Establishing rules. Involve the class in devising a set of speaking and listening rules. Discuss and evaluate all suggestions for appropriate behaviour. Record and display choices on speaking and listening charts.

> **When I speak I**
> - stand on my spot
> - look at the class
> - work out what I shall say

- Courteous listening. Discuss factors that contribute to effective, courteous listening, e.g. with a partner, in a group, as a whole class, at assembly. Focus on listening behaviours during selected activities and encourage children to reflect on and evaluate their own listening skills.

- Working cooperatively. Encourage children to become active participants in their own learning and develop social skills through a range of cooperative projects:
  - write a class newspaper
  - prepare a school camp report
  - complete a shared mathematics activity
  - produce a puppet play
  - design a game
  - plan an assembly item.

- Excursions and visits. Excursions outside the school broaden children's general knowledge and expose them to a range of language styles. Visit areas of interest in the immediate neighbourhood, e.g. shopping centres, community store, health centre, retirement village. Establish a specific purpose for visits by discussing and planning information to be obtained, how it will be used, people to interview, questions to ask, photographs to take.

Language and Literacy

(See p. 66)

Speaking, listening, reading and writing are interrelated and each has a role in communication. Children need to understand how each complements the others and how development in one area is linked to development in the others. They should be given opportunities to discuss literature, make comparisons between oral and written language and extend their range and use of vocabulary across all curriculum areas.

The *Oral Language: Resource Book* chapter *Language and Literacy* outlines strategies and skills for developing literacy understandings through oral language.

- Newstelling. Newstelling requires children to recall, sequence and summarise experiences or events for presentation to an audience. Encourage children to elaborate on information and include topic-specific vocabulary. Assist planning through a news framework that includes the elements *when, who, where, what, why*.

Vary grouping from partner to small group to whole class. This approach places different demands on the way children plan and present information. When children are familiar with the planning process, introduce other oral language forms, e.g. descriptions, explanations, reports, procedures.

- Linking newstelling into writing. Discuss how the elements of a recount are similar for oral or written texts, i.e. *when, who, where, what, why*. Demonstrate how a news plan can be used to prepare written texts. Brainstorm words or phrases under key headings and use the information to write a recount.

when	who	where	what	why
Sunday	Mum Dad me brother	beach Albany	swim fish	day off work Dad

- Topic news. Use the newstelling framework to plan and present information related to personal interests, holidays, family etc.

- School news. Gather and prepare information based on school or classroom events. Present weekly reports and encourage the audience to ask questions, add comments or take notes for a class newspaper.

- Oral sharing activities. Introduce sharing times after classroom activities, e.g. art and crafts, mathematics, social studies. Provide appropriate frameworks for planning and presenting information.

> ## Tell Us What You Made.
> - What is it called?
> - What does it look like?
> - What can you do with it?
> - What do you like about it?

- News reports. Collect samples of newspaper reports and make overhead transparencies. Have the children identify the key elements *when, who, where, what, why*. When children are familiar with the procedure, introduce independent analysis of news reports. Use the information to summarise and present oral reports to the class. Encourage children to express an opinion or draw conclusions from the text.

- News pictures. Use photographs or illustrations to generate oral news reports. Provide headings or key words to assist planning. Encourage children to interpret the photograph from their own point of view and justify their opinions.

On Monday a ship ran aground off...

- Presenting to different audiences. Present oral recounts or reports to a variety of audiences, e.g. other classes, parents, assemblies.

- Using news to entertain. Have children select a personal experience or news report and develop it into a 'tall story'. Discuss the humour of the stories, language used and features which make them tall stories.
- Distinguishing fact from opinion. Record newspaper articles on overhead transparencies. Discuss the content and help children to distinguish fact from opinion.
- 'Show and Tell' news. Introduce activities that assist children to use and extend their use of descriptive language. Display a description chart and add or delete attribute or function words to suit the topic, e.g. *size, colour, shape, texture, how it's used, who uses it*. Encourage children to use subject-specific vocabulary during oral and written news sessions.
- News tape exchange. Prepare and exchange news tapes related to classroom, school or community events. Encourage children to add opinions or evaluative comments to motivate a reaction from the audience. Discuss the need to make information more explicit for the listener.
- Sharing knowledge. Organise pairs or groups to research and report on curriculum-related topics. Provide books, magazines, journals, newspaper etc. Display a framework to assist planning and presentation:
  - What is the topic?
  - Where did you find information?
  - What did you discover?
- Enjoying literature. Expose children to a range of books that promotes enjoyment, e.g. traditional stories, cumulative texts, books featuring rhyme and repetition, poetry. Encourage children to compare and express opinions on different styles, authors and illustrators.
- Telling stories. Tell stories without the aid of written text or illustrations. This approach motivates children to create their own image of the characters and events. Discuss children's interpretations of the story and provide follow-up activities to demonstrate understandings:
  - draw one event and describe it to a friend
  - draw a character and describe it to the group
  - make a story map
  - retell the story in a circle by adding on to the previous speaker's contribution.

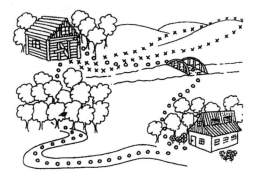

- Storytelling variations. Tell a story and have children work in groups to prepare a retell that includes some variation, e.g. different setting, new character added, character omitted, added event. Tell the new stories and compare and evaluate variations.
- Linking storytelling to writing. Tell a story and have the children retell their interpretation in a variety of ways:
  - write a retell
  - illustrate and write about one event
  - work in groups, allocate events, write the text and present the completed story to the class.
- Textless books. Work in groups to generate a story from a textless book. Discuss and reach consensus on an appropriate storyline before assigning writing tasks. This activity is also suitable for oral retells.
- Retelling stories. Read a story and have children retell their version individually or in groups. Alternatively, add or delete a character, setting or event.
- Telling stories in sequence. Prepare sets of pictures relating to a familiar story. Have children work in groups to sequence the pictures and prepare a retell. Make the strategy more challenging by introducing unfamiliar sets of pictures. Children must express opinions, show a knowledge of story structure and reach consensus to sequence the pictures. Have each group tell its story version, then compare and evaluate the effectiveness of each variation.
- Interviewing characters. Conduct a shared book session with a traditional or unfamiliar story. Discuss each character's motives and role in the story. Brainstorm questions that will elicit each character's point of view. Nominate children to role play the characters while the remainder of the class conducts an interview.

- Expressing viewpoints. Have children role play characters from traditional stories or fables. Each character tells the story from his or her point of view. Discuss the power of language to persuade, e.g. use of voice, choice of words, emotive expressions.
- Circle stories. Conduct a shared book session. Discuss setting, characters, events, conclusion. Model how to create a progressive story by taking turns to add to and develop the previous speaker's contribution. Work in groups to retell the story, then discuss the importance

of listening to the developing storyline before adding a logical extension. Make the activity more challenging by providing 'story starters' to introduce a spontaneous story. Props may include pictures, character profiles, a setting, puppets, masks etc.

- Talking about stories. Listen to stories written by other children. Focus on the language used and evaluate its effectiveness in conveying meaning. Discuss and experiment with language that may alter or clarify the intended message.

- Shared reading. Conduct shared reading sessions. Discuss how stories, poems, plays etc. can be expressed through oral or written forms.

- Speculative questions. After literature activities, formulate and ask speculative questions to stimulate discussion and elicit different opinions and ideas. Include *who, what, when, why, how* questions.

- Identifying main idea. Cover the title of an informational text. Look through the contents of the book and ask children to suggest titles. Justify suggestions, discuss them and compare final choice with the actual title.

- Identifying cause and effect. Listen to stories and ask questions such as *What if ... had/hadn't happened? Why do you think ...? How would you feel if ...?*

- Developing vocabulary. Help children to extend the range of words used and understood, and to incorporate more specialised vocabulary, where appropriate.

- Brainstorming. Brainstorm and record ideas and vocabulary. Discuss the importance of using specialised vocabulary to enhance meaning.

- Terminology. Introduce, chart and discuss subject-specific vocabulary in all curriculum areas. Provide opportunities to practise correct terminology through oral reports, discussion, interviews, explanations etc.

- Descriptive language. Introduce activities that place a focus on description, e.g. describing an accident, person, experience, object. Discuss the importance of using language that assists the listener to form an accurate image of the event or item being described.

- Modelled writing. Conduct modelled writing sessions that assist children to make the links between oral and written forms.

- Linking narrative to writing. Write character studies, retell stories, rewrite a narrative as a play, comic strip, poem etc. Encourage the children to work in groups to share ideas, write, edit and produce a final copy.

- Writing instructions. Write instructions for others to complete a task, e.g. conducting a science experiment, cooking, making a model, completing a mathematics activity. Discuss reasons for misinterpretations and devise rules for conveying explicit information:
  – provide sufficient detail
  – use correct vocabulary
  – provide a logical sequence.

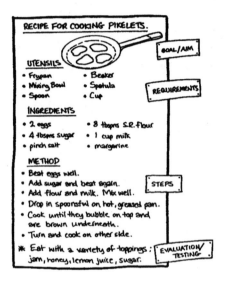

Language and Thinking

(See p. 66)

Children are curious and enthusiastic about learning. As they encounter different experiences they experiment, explore, make discoveries and form hypotheses. They use language to clarify and extend their thinking, then communicate their understandings to others. At this stage, children should be given many opportunities to use language to develop logical thinking, to investigate problems in meaningful situations and to demonstrate what they know about the world around them.

The *Oral Language: Resource Book* chapter *Language and Thinking* outlines strategies and activities for developing cognitive skills.

- Demonstrating knowledge. An effective method for demonstrating understandings or knowledge of a topic is through telling someone else about it—peers, teachers or other adults. Organise sessions to include sharing times, either during or after the activity. This approach motivates children to monitor what they are doing, to reflect on the activity and to select the most pertinent information for the listener. Initially, provide support by modelling how to plan and present information:
  - outline the purpose for sharing
  - describe what has been produced
  - explain how it was produced
  - provide an evaluative comment.
- Problem solving. Children develop thinking skills when they use language to experiment, explore and solve problems. Take time to create open-ended tasks that can be approached in different ways and which have a range of solutions. Focus on the language involved in thinking through the process rather than aiming to find only one correct answer. Encourage children to explore together, experiment, observe, discuss and express their understandings to peers and adults:
  - complete manipulative puzzles, solve riddles and brain-teasers
  - work with a partner to draw a procedure from written instructions
  - work in a group to write instructions from illustrations
  - invent and describe the thinking behind the design for a simple machine
  - investigate mathematical problems together and brainstorm a range of solutions
  - follow more complex instructions to locate positions on a map.
- Writing in groups. Problems are easier to solve when children can share their thoughts and ideas with others. Organise partner or group activities where children must talk together to complete the task. When children interact they use language to refine their thinking skills,

demonstrate and explain processes to others, or explore possibilities through discussion, questioning and observation:
  - solve mathematical problems together
  - discuss controversial issues in small groups before presenting opinions to class
  - work with a partner to conduct and present findings from an experiment
  - write and perform a play together
  - practise and present a cumulative story.
- Finding solutions. Introduce some activities with a question, e.g. *How long will it take an ice-cube to melt? What are some methods of keeping time?* Motivate the children to work and talk together to find solutions. Include a sharing time in which children recall and reflect on the processes involved in the task.
- Science. Before science investigations, give children opportunities to predict, hypothesise and brainstorm possible outcomes or solutions. When children talk about what they see they clarify their observations.

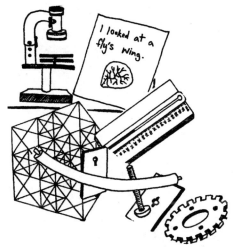

Talking also enables questions to be asked. Considering these questions leads to further investigations as children become actively involved in discovering new information:
  - encourage children to talk before investigations
  - work in groups to share ideas, predictions and explanations

- include a sharing time at the end of activities for verifying predictions, explaining solutions and evaluating group participation.
- Mathematics. Introduce mathematical activities that develop concepts and vocabulary in meaningful situations. Provide open-ended tasks that encourage children to predict outcomes and link previous experiences to new situations:
  - work with a partner to estimate, then check, solutions
  - work together to provide a 2-D or 3-D representation of a problem
  - work with a partner to brainstorm and experiment with different means of depicting information, e.g. drawing, diagram, graph
  - identify and describe patterns to a partner, e.g. number patterns, shape patterns
  - have children restate the problem to a peer or adult.
- Classification. Assist children to develop thinking skills by classifying what they observe, know, read or discuss:
  - provide topic-related pictures, items or texts and have children sort them according to their own rules
  - nominate the criteria for sorting, e.g. words with one syllable, two syllables, three syllables
  - work with a partner to sort pictures or information for a graph
  - classify pictures or information using semantic grids
  - classify storybook characters according to personalities, actions, motives.
- Planning. Involve children in planning and organising classroom activities, excursions or school camps. Encourage children to relate discussions to past experiences, to predict what they might see or do, to help plan the activities, and to compare the experience with their predictions.
- Questioning. Model how to ask questions to clarify and gain information or analyse and explore ideas. Teach children the question words—*when, who, where, what, why*—that elicit different types of information.

WHAT?

WHO?   WHY?

WHERE?   HOW?

WHEN?

Introduce activities that motivate children to practise questioning skills:
- have children work in groups to plan interview questions
- introduce open-ended tasks that motivate children to question and explore a range of solutions
- demonstrate how to ask open questions that allow for a range of interpretations and responses

- model how to elicit information from a partner through literal and inferential questions.

Wait for children to question instead of providing them with immediate information.
- Teacher's questions. Avoid asking questions that elicit only closed responses. Questions should be sufficiently challenging to raise the level of children's thinking and promote learning:
  - ask questions that require children to provide information or clarify their thinking during problem-solving activities
  - question to stimulate and extend thinking, e.g. by asking for alternative solutions, another opinion, a more elaborated explanation
  - help children to reflect on their thinking, e.g. by explaining how they solved a problem, completed a task.
- Reading. Read a variety of literature and ask questions that motivate children to think about the text:
  - describe details – *what, when, who, where, why*
  - recognise main idea

  - identify and describe supporting details
  - describe sequences
  - recognise cause and effect
  - identify character traits.
- Expressing feelings. Provide children with opportunities to express their feelings:
  - respond to music and literature
  - talk about things that make them sad, happy, excited
  - express opinions about people, books, experiences.
- Listening. Provide opportunities to listen for a variety of purposes. When children have something to listen *for*, rather than listen *to*, more active learning takes place:
  - ask children questions before a story to provide a focus for listening
  - organise activities where children must listen and make judgments, e.g. debates, panel discussions, interviews
  - encourage children to listen and draw inferences from TV reports, radio reports, debates
  - have group discussions that focus on perceptive listening, e.g. 'reading between the lines'
  - include activities which focus on listening and responding to more complex sequences of instructions.

For Parents

How can I help my child with speaking and listening?

- Set aside 10-15 minutes to discuss what has happened during the day.
- Involve your child in conversations, plans and discussions.
- Ask and answer questions.
- Encourage your child to express and justify opinions, develop logical arguments, and give reasons for decisions made.
- Involve your child in adult conversations, when appropriate. These experiences will help develop an awareness of how they and others use language.
- Provide a good listening model by showing interest in, and responding to, your child's contributions. For example, use mealtimes for discussion and encourage all family members to participate.
- Talk about topics of mutual interest and expect that your child will listen and respond.
- Provide a wide variety of books such as traditional stories, magazines, comics, atlases, dictionaries and reference books.
- Read serials or short stories.
- Encourage your child to read for pleasure.
- Compare similarities and differences between a book your child has read and its movie version, e.g. *Chitty Chitty Bang Bang* or *Winnie The Pooh*.
- Talk about current affairs viewed on television. If possible, find and read the corresponding newspaper reports.
- If your child shows an interest in a television or sports personality, make a note of any photographs or newspaper reports. Read and discuss the information with your child.
- Talk about special events or family celebrations. Encourage your child to create cards, invitations or greetings.
- Encourage your child to practise a variety of writing forms such as letters, lists and messages.
- When your child asks how to spell a word, encourage a 'have-a-go first' approach.
- Play language games such as 'I Spy' and 'Hang the Man'.
- Play commercial games which focus on word building or word knowledge.
- Include the family in games which provide enjoyment and teach social skills, e.g. taking turns, explaining rules to another player, congratulating the winner.
- Encourage your child to entertain the family with simple plays, puppet shows or jokes.

- Ask your child to recount and evaluate experiences, e.g. weekly Tee-ball or football matches.
- Involve your child in planning for holidays. Provide such items such as road maps, travel brochures, a calendar, and paper and pencils for making lists, writing reminders etc.
- Show your child how to locate a street or suburb using a street directory.
- Teach your child how to use a telephone, and locate names in a directory.
- Use your local library.

Extended Language for Learning

In this phase speakers/listeners continue to extend and refine their understandings and use of language. Language is manipulated and adapted to suit a range of audiences and purposes.

Sample of newstelling: Michael (Year 6)

… and we divided into four groups called the Settlers, the Miners, the Shopkeepers and the Explorers and we each took turns at acting out scenes and we each had a different chore to do and we stayed there till Tuesday. Just before lunch, and after lunch for a while, we got to spend our pocket money that we saved up and had given to Mrs Simpson before we actually went there and we, and I bought some, some marbles, a key ring and a bottle of, well, a very small bottle of friendship beads at the toyshop. And, um, apparently, I didn't actually know anything but I was told that on Monday night, um, when everybody was asleep, I actually slept walked and, um, so a few things happened then which, um, we all had a good laugh about …

Assessing Michael's Oral Language

- ◆ **sustains appropriate language and style, e.g. formal, informal talk**
- ◆ **effectively interprets whether a message has been understood**
- is aware of audience and purpose
- confidently and competently recounts events, providing detail and elaboration
- shows advanced planning of content when presenting information, e.g. in reports, summaries
- selects vocabulary for impact, e.g. to persuade, surprise

The teacher's observations during this newstelling session and other interactive activities indicate that Michael is in the *Extended Language for Learning* phase.

Extended Language for Learning Indicators

Language of Social Interaction

(See p. 83)

The speaker/listener:

◆ **selects and sustains language and style appropriate to purpose, context and audience, e.g. formal, informal talk**
◆ **effectively interprets whether a message has been understood**
- takes into account another's point of view, e.g. *from your point of view this might be expensive but the benefits for the animals are of vital importance.*
- needs and uses language to moderate or reduce the conflict
- uses appropriate social conventions
- is aware of audience and purpose, e.g. 'This presentation is on the history of mining in this area. As you already know about early exploration, I will not go into too much detail about events prior to 1880'
- refines use of appropriate facial expressions and gestures to communicate ideas, feelings and information.

Language and Literacy

(See p. 86)

The speaker/listener:

◆ **summarises main ideas from written or spoken texts using succinct language**
◆ **draws conclusions from, makes inferences based on and evaluates written and oral text and is able to listen and respond to an alternative perspective**
◆ **describes events, objects and concepts outside immediate experience, e.g. world news**
- shows advanced planning of content when presenting information, e.g. in reports, summaries
- selects vocabulary for impact, e.g. to persuade, surprise
- uses language to reflect on and discuss written or spoken texts
- confidently and competently recounts events, providing detail and elaboration
- demonstrates fluency and a personal style when reading orally
- discusses rules of language, grammar.

Language and Thinking

(See p. 89)

The speaker/listener:

◆ **uses language to express independent, critical thinking**
◆ **uses oral language to formulate hypotheses, criticise, evaluate, plan and to influence the thinking of others**
◆ **deals with abstract ideas using concrete examples**
- listens to the ideas and viewpoints of others, using oral language to respond, expressing and modifying own opinions
- presents a variety of arguments to support a claim
- compares and contrasts observations, ideas, hypotheses with others
- explains understandings of topics, concepts, etc. providing convincing argument and evidence to support point of view
- recognises potential and limitations of words to persuade, explain, clarify, solve problems etc.
- answers spontaneous questions in an informed, competent manner, making sure that listeners understand what is being said
- uses language to paint 'word pictures'.

The recent mini series shown on Channel 4 was a fascinating account of life on the Goldfields.

Teaching Notes

In this phase, students will continue to develop an understanding of language and its many uses.

Teachers need to help students develop proficiency in speaking and listening so they communicate effectively and efficiently. Emphasis should be placed on clear speech and a logical and fluent expression of ideas. Students should also extend and specialise their use of vocabulary when communicating their ideas and understandings.

Continue to encourage students to use appropriate methods of communication in a variety of situations and for a variety of purposes. For example:

- to express and justify feelings and opinions with increasing sophistication during social studies discussions
- to discuss increasingly complex issues related to current affairs
- to recount experiences and events in and out of school
- to present ideas and understandings in a widening range of contexts across the curriculum
- to present factual information clearly and logically during debates
- to discriminate between fact and opinion in newspaper articles
- to give increasingly precise instructions during science activities
- to respond to increasingly complex instructions and questions during reading comprehension
- to listen and respond to an increasing range of fiction, non-fiction, plays and poetry
- to predict the outcome and compare the result of an experiment.

Promote a positive attitude to speaking and listening by encouraging students to share their feelings and experiences through discussion and group activities. In this phase, students should be involved in evaluating and adapting their speaking and listening behaviours in response to the increasingly complex demands of the curriculum. They should also begin to develop an awareness of the power of the spoken word to influence or control human behaviour.

Major Teaching Emphases

- **structure experiences that challenge students to select and use different styles of language to suit a range of audiences and purposes**
- **help students to develop proficient speaking and listening skills that focus on clear speech, and a logical and sequential expression of ideas and understandings**
- **promote the use of subject-specific vocabulary**

- include activities and resources that encourage students to reflect on the aesthetic features of language
- involve the students in planning presentations, e.g. to the class, school assembly
- structure activities to enable students to interpret, summarise or evaluate a range of texts
- help students to develop language for independent, critical thinking
- provide opportunities for students to use langauge to persuade, surprise, entertain or amuse others
- help students to give and respond to increasingly complex explanations and instructions

At all phases:
- **provide models of correct English**
- ensure that students encounter a range of purposes, audiences and situations that challenge them to use language in many different ways
- **allow time to practise the sounds, rhythms, words and structures of language**
- **make links between oral and written language**
- encourage students to respond to a range of oral and visual texts
- **value the processes of group interaction.**

- *Entries in bold are considered critical to the children's further development*

Establishing an Environment for Speaking and Listening

Speaking and listening are part of the whole learning process and cannot be developed in isolation. Students should see oral language as an integral and important component of all curriculum-related experiences. They should be given opportunities to become more competent and confident in using oral language effectively and efficiently for a variety of purposes, in different situations. When students know that what they have to say will be listened to and valued, they will feel more confident to express their ideas, understandings, opinions and feelings.

Ways to Create an Environment for Speaking and Listening

- Consider the classroom as an environment for encouraging oral language development. Organise situations and activities in which students can:
  - work with other students to discuss, listen to and exchange ideas
  - develop speaking and listening skills
  - have direct experiences
  - learn from others who have had different experiences
  - find answers to their own questions
  - talk about what they learn.
- Create a classroom that motivates students to speak and interact with a range of teachers, other adults, and peers.
- Encourage students to use language for learning in all curriculum areas.
- Stimulate students to engage in purposeful conversation by introducing topics, highlighting issues, presenting problems or displaying relevant pictures. Discuss and practise appropriate social courtesies, e.g. listening to others, respecting different opinions, asking pertinent questions.
- Introduce informal debates or panel discussions to assist children to form and express opinions related to current issues or curriculum-related topics.
- Organise discussion groups and encourage students to become actively involved as speakers and listeners. Provide opportunities to exchange opinions, clarify thinking, gain new knowledge and express ideas.
- Encourage students to assume teaching roles through peer tutoring activities. This will motivate students to clarify and consolidate their own understandings before they attempt to explain or demonstrate a skill to others.
- Engage students in role plays based on either real or imagined experiences. Students' language will become more extended and expressive as they learn to project into the experiences, actions and feelings of others.

- Include an area for the whole class to gather for sharing ideas, conducting discussions and introducing literature.
- Establish a class library that contains a variety of reading materials. Encourage students to share information about favourite authors and topics.
- Continue shared book activities. Include both fictional and informational texts. Encourage students to discuss and compare different formats, illustrations, authors and styles.
- Engage students in oral retells of familiar and unfamiliar stories.
- Build up a poetry collection. Read and recite poems that motivate students to enjoy the sounds and rhythms of the English language. Choose poetry to support classroom themes, to reflect cultural backgrounds, or to provide insights into different styles or forms.
- Introduce choral speaking to help recreate the mood and meaning of different poems.
- Introduce puppetry as a strategy for interpreting literature, e.g. write a script from a story text, produce puppets and present a play.
- Include drama activities that allow students to express their ideas and listen to the ideas of others.
- Work with students to provide a print-rich environment. Discuss the different purposes for writing.
- Display and talk about subject-specific vocabulary. Extend understandings of word use through crosswords, rhebus activities, word sleuths or other word study activities.
- Provide a selection of commercial and class-made word games. Supply dictionaries and other resources to develop and extend word knowledge.

Language of Social Interaction

(See p. 79)

Students develop an increased awareness of the social roles of speaking and listening when they are involved in real-life situations that allow them to explore and modify their beliefs, values, attitudes and emotions. Through interaction with a wide range of audiences, students learn to listen and respond courteously, respect others' opinions and develop an awareness of the effects of language in influencing or directing human behaviour.

Teachers should provide students with many opportunities to practise and adjust language styles to suit particular purposes and audiences. They should also demonstrate appropriate models of courtesy, respect and polite behaviour. In an environment in which they know that what they have to say will be listened to and valued, students will be more inclined to respect and tolerate the ideas, opinions and needs of others.

The *Oral Language: Resource Book* chapter *Language of Social Interaction* provides strategies and activities that assist students to adapt language for many purposes and audiences.

The following activities and groupings promote appropriate and effective communication skills across all curriculum areas.

- Peers. Provide opportunities for students to discuss issues, express opinions and develop an understanding of the power of language to influence and manipulate the behaviour of others.
  - discuss controversial issues, e.g. pollution, smoking, woodchipping. Research and compile information about methods used to influence the public, e.g. advertising, marches, posters, interviews.
  - make students familiar with methods used to persuade people through radio or television commercials, e.g. to listen to or watch programs, buy products, support media personalities.
  - listen to poems, stories, news items, advertisements, and locate words and phrases used to arouse certain feelings in the listener. Discuss reasons why such words may or may not achieve the desired effect. Identify other strategies for generating emotive responses, e.g. use of voice, emphasis, volume, exclamation, questions, non-verbal behaviours.
- Encourage students to interact with familiar and unfamiliar peers. Unfamiliar groups place more challenging demands on the way students plan and use language:
  - organise peer tutoring of younger children
  - report completed activities to another class
  - explain how to play a new game
  - outline procedures for cooking

  - conduct reading sessions with younger children
  - take responsibility for running assemblies with another class.
- Student to teacher. Promote appropriate language styles by facilitating, rather than monopolising, talk in the classroom:
  - encourage students to talk to and with teachers
  - motivate students to listen critically to and ask questions of teachers
  - include activities that encourage students to hypothesise, speculate and express opinions
  - provide students with opportunities to respond to ideas or actions.
- Small groups. Group size influences the type and effectiveness of interactions in the classroom. To ensure maximum benefit from group work, introduce activities that challenge students to extend language use beyond informal chatter.

> ＊ Work in groups to decide the five most important arguments against smoking.
> ＊ Prepare an oral report for the class.

- Small-group problem solving. Have the students work together to solve a problem by consensus, e.g. finding a solution to traffic in front of the school or planning an appropriate timetable for school camp. Attempt to solve the problem in different ways:
  - brainstorm good and bad aspects

- list possible solutions
- speculate on consequences
- explore, discuss and present solutions to others.

Let's list all the bad points about smoking first.

- Sharing information. In this group strategy, each child receives part of the information required to complete a task. Students take turns to share their information with the group, which then decides where each section belongs in the whole:
  - order chunks of a poem, song, recipe
  - sequence information to follow directions at a school camp
  - sequence literature-related illustrations and text
  - order speech balloons to complete a cartoon.
- Ranking. In groups, students consider priorities for given information. Final ranking must be decided through discussion and joint consensus:
  - rank results of a health survey
  - suggest and rank criteria for being a successful politician
  - study community services and rank in perceived order of importance
  - record rankings of most important school rules.
- Brainstorming. Organise groups to share ideas about classroom topics. Have students accept all ideas and withhold discussion until ideas are exhausted. Review, delete or classify ideas through group discussion:
  - important/irrelevant information
  - needs further discussion.
  Share decisions with whole class. Encourage students to discuss and evaluate social behaviours that support or impede this type of group activity.
- Save the last word for me. This strategy prevents one or two students from dominating the group. Provide each student with a copy of a poem, story, transcript of an interview etc. Instruct them to read silently and underline their favourite section. The first student then identifies and explains reasons for his/her choice. The speaker must then remain silent while other group members comment on the selection. The speaker has last right of reply before the next child repeats the process.
- Envoy. Introduce and discuss a topic in small groups. One student from each group is then chosen to be the 'envoy', who will report to another group about the discussion—ideas, suggestions, conclusions, decisions etc. Each envoy reports to a host group, listens to that group's discussion points and reports this information

back to the original group. Use the envoy strategy in all curriculum areas.

- Jigsaws. Introduce and discuss a curriculum-related topic. Organise 'home' groups and assign a different number to each student in a group: 1, 2, 3, … All students with identical numbers form 'expert' groups that investigate a specific aspect of the topic, e.g. climate, occupations, transport, physical features, industry. Each group prepares a report on the topic, then individuals return to their home group to share the information.

Peter knew a lot of facts about the desert. He said …

- Pair to four. This activity assists students to share knowledge and develop discussion skills. Organise partners and assign a task, e.g. work on a mathematics problem, share what is known or has been learned about a topic. Set a time limit and stress the importance of each person having equal opportunities to speak. At the end of the allocated time ask each pair to form a group with another pair. One student from each pair then reports information obtained from the partner. This approach motivates students to listen carefully during the initial discussion, to question for clarification, to summarise information, and to present a planned and logical report to the other group.
- Discussion. Organise whole-class and small-group discussion in a range of subject areas. Through

discussion, students develop social skills and learn content and vocabulary more thoroughly. Include:
- all groups discussing one topic
- all groups discussing a different topic
- the class discussing different aspects of a topic
- whole-class discussion preceding small-group discussion.

Organise discussion groups so that students are actively engaged as speakers and listeners. Choice of topics should assist students to reach a deeper understanding of issues through argument, debate or conversation. Students should also understand that the outcome of a discussion is not necessarily one correct answer, but rather an exchange of ideas and opinions as issues are explored.

At this stage, students should be able to discuss home, neighbourhood and world events and issues:
- discuss social issues such as unemployment, health problems, alcohol-related traffic accidents
- include students' immediate interests and issues, e.g. peer pressure, family issues
- establish a class council to discuss issues that arise within the classroom
- discuss emotive issues such as poverty, war.

- Panel discussions. Develop or review topics that invite discussion and expression of different opinions. Organise a panel comprising several speakers and a chairperson, who invites questions from the audience and allocates them to particular speakers. Discuss the importance of interpreting the question, selecting key elements to support a response, and presenting the information in a suitably persuasive manner.

- Informal debates. Informal debates are similar to open discussions in which all students are involved in presenting and justifying their opinions and supporting or opposing the opinions of others.

- Formal debating. Formal debating combines the skills of public speaking and argument with the aim of persuading an audience. The success of a debate depends on thorough preparation and good teamwork. A formal debate involves:
- a topic which is presented in the affirmative
- an affirmative team of three speakers to support the topic
- a negative team of three speakers to oppose the topic
- a chairperson to run the debate
- a timekeeper to control the time
- an adjudicator to judge individual speakers and team performances and award the final marks or results.

Initially, aim to develop a knowledge of debating procedure before focusing on content. Later, encourage clear, logical and persuasive argument from the speakers, and have time for constructive criticism to reflect on the issues.

- Meetings. Teach formal meeting procedures through class or school councils. Begin by making all participants familiar with the appropriate rules and procedures:
- have short class meetings to decide on issues such as class rules, behaviour, class trips, school camp
- role play situations such as school student meetings, sporting club meetings and political meetings
- establish a class council, elect office bearers and introduce classroom issues for debate or discussion.

- Establishing rules. Involve the class in devising a set of speaking and listening rules. Discuss and evaluate all suggestions for appropriate behaviour. Record and display choices on speaking and listening charts.

- Courteous listening. Discuss factors that contribute to effective, courteous listening, e.g. when interacting with a partner, in a group, as a whole class. Focus on listening behaviours during selected activities and encourage students to reflect on and evaluate their own listening skills.

- Conversation. Introduce topics, resources and displays that motivate students to engage in spontaneous or directed conversation. In the classroom, purposeful conversation is ensured when topics are of genuine interest and within the realms of students' experience. Include current events, issues, problems or concerns. Reflect on appropriate social behaviours such as listening carefully, acknowledging different opinions, responding courteously.

- Working cooperatively. Encourage students to become active participants in their own learning and to develop social skills through a range of cooperative tasks:
- preparing a class meeting
- writing a class newspaper
- interviewing a community member
- completing a mathematical activity
- writing and producing a puppet play
- designing a game
- planning an assembly item.

- Excursions and visits. Expose students to a range of language styles and social contexts through excursions and visits. Include visits within the school, in the immediate neighbourhood and in the wider community. Establish a specific purpose for the visit and incorporate activities that involve speaking and listening, e.g. interviews, oral history, discussion, video, research. Use collected information as a basis for further activities in the classroom.

Language and Literacy

(See p. 79)
Students at this phase should demonstrate control over a wide range of oral forms, e.g. recount, report, summary, explanation. Their abilities to evaluate, plan and present information orally have a direct effect on the way they use language to read and write. Students need to be given many opportunities to engage in meaningful tasks that integrate speaking, listening, reading and writing across the curriculum.

The *Oral Language: Resource Book* chapter *Language and Literacy* outlines activities and strategies for developing literacy understandings through oral language.

- Newstelling. Newstelling requires students to recall, sequence and summarise experiences or events for presentation to an audience. Encourage students to provide sufficient elaboration and detail to satisfy the demands of the audience. Vary grouping from partner to small group, to class. This approach allows students to move from informal to more formal presentations.

- Topic news. Include news sessions that are linked to community or world events. Discuss the topics and encourage students to carry out further research, collect newspaper articles or watch TV reports.

- School news. Gather and prepare information linked to classroom or school events. Present weekly reports and incorporate a questioning or review component.

- Oral sharing. Introduce a sharing time at the conclusion of nominated activities, e.g. after group activities involving mathematics, science experiments, art and craft. Encourage students to describe both the product and process of the activity, i.e. the outcomes and how they were achieved. At this stage, students should also add an evaluative comment about successes, difficulties experienced or advantages of working with a partner.

- News reports. Prepare samples of newspaper reports on overheads. Have students identify the key elements, *when, who, where, what, why*. Work with a partner to produce a summary that includes all key elements. Use the summary to present an oral report to the class. When the students are familiar with the procedure, have them write news reports from TV or radio reports.

- News pictures. Use photographs or illustrations to generate oral or written news reports. Provide planning frameworks with the headings *when, who, where, what, why*. Information generated can be used for either a summary or more elaborate report.

The following activities are designed to help students understand the language features and structure of narrative texts as they work with or create their own texts. The activities move from an oral to a written focus and place an emphasis on partner or small-group work. Students are encouraged to use talk as a tool for developing ideas, clarifying understandings and generating cohesive narrative texts.

- Enjoying literature. Expose students to a range of texts that promote enjoyment and entertainment, e.g. traditional stories, fables, myths, cumulative stories, poems, plays.

- Telling stories. Storytelling is different from story-reading. With storytelling, both speaker and listener create a mental picture from the words. The storyteller's face, voice, personality and body help to convey mood and meaning. Story-reading, on the other hand, relies on the text and illustrations to enhance meaning. The reader is constrained by the framework, format and text of the story.

Tell a wide range of stories to the students before asking them to engage in their own storytelling. Discuss plot, setting, style, characters, theme etc.

- Video frame. Tell a story and ask students to freeze one event. Draw the action and describe that part of the story to a partner.

- Story interpretation. Tell a story and have students:
  - visualise and draw one of the characters. Compare and discuss the illustrations
  - retell the story around a circle by adding on to the previous speaker's contribution.

- Group stories. Tell stories to different class groups. Have each group practise and retell the story to another group.

- Round-robin stories. Tell a story to a small group. That group retells it to another group and so on around the class. Discuss and compare the final version with the original.

- Visiting storytellers. Invite a visitor to tell a story. The students retell the story to another class.
- Story commissions. Ask one group to commission another group to create a story with specified setting and characters.

- Storytelling variations. Tell a story and have students work in groups to prepare a retell that includes some variation, e.g. different setting, new character added, sad ending, different point of view. Present then compare effectiveness of variations.
- Written retells. Storytelling helps students to read and write because it gives them frameworks for understanding text. When students have a 'sense of story' they can apply this knowledge to their own reading, writing and storytelling:
  - write an individual retell of a story
  - write a group retell
  - write a retell that includes specified changes, e.g. different hero, time, setting, dialogue etc.
  - write a retell in a different text form, e.g. play, poem, limerick.
- Textless books. Work in groups to generate a story from a textless book. Have students discuss the illustrations and reach consensus on an appropriate story-line before preparing an oral or written version of the story. Compare each group's contribution.
- Sequence stories. Prepare sets of pictures relating to an unfamiliar story. Have students work in groups to sequence the pictures and prepare an oral or written retell. Make the activity more challenging by providing open-ended pictures that can be sequenced in a variety of ways. This approach places greater demands on the group to work together to create a logical story-line.

- Interviewing characters. Conduct a shared book session and discuss the characters' motives and role in the story. Brainstorm interview questions that may elicit each character's point of view. Nominate students to role play the characters and answer any questions directed from the audience.
- Predicting informational texts. Cover the title and ask students to describe the cover and suggest a title. List responses. Look through the contents of the book and give students the opportunity to change their suggestions. Compare title with list.
- Creating text. Have students work in pairs to write text using only the illustrations or diagrams as the source of information. Initially, each child may write independently before comparing the text with a partner. At the conclusion of the activity, compare all versions with that of the book.

- Developing vocabulary. Help students to extend the range of words used and understood, and to incorporate more specialised vocabulary in speaking and writing. Encourage students to manipulate words, discover word origins and experience enjoyment in using more interesting or sophisticated terminology.
- Brainstorming. Brainstorm and record vocabulary as new topics are introduced. Make charts of the most appropriate words and encourage students to use them in both oral and written texts.

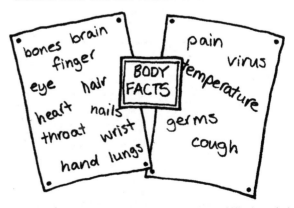

- Modelled and shared writing. Use modelled and shared writing to demonstrate how to select and use more precise vocabulary. Discuss word meanings, choice of correct terminology and impact of different words in influencing the reader.

- Dictionary skills. Work with a partner then share discoveries with the class:
  - find the meanings of words encountered in reading or discussion activities
  - find all the meanings of common words, e.g. table, slide, run, bank
  - devise rules for a given crossword puzzle or design a puzzle
  - use a thesaurus to find a set of synonyms in a set time
  - classify a list of words according to origin.
- Fun with words. Select unusual or interesting words from stories, rhymes, poems, songs etc. Encourage students to use them as a focus in creating their own stories or poems:
  - find onomatopoeic words that have been created to echo sounds, e.g. hiss, buzz, clank, click-clack
  - classify words according to meaning; length, letter patterns, initial sounds, etc.
  - find antonyms and synonyms
  - write shape words, e.g. *ice, tall, scary*
  - illustrate idioms, e.g. *raining cats and dogs.*

'Raining Cats and Dogs'

The following activities are designed to help students plan and present information with the purpose of persuading or influencing others.

- Argue the case. Each week choose a topic for discussion. Topics related to subject areas will have more relevance and impact. Organise groups and provide each with a sheet of paper folded down the middle. Write YES on one side and NO on the other. Spend five to ten minutes producing arguments for and against the topic.
- Campaigning. Run a classroom election, e.g. as part of a study of local government or parliamentary procedures. Speakers must prepare and deliver a speech that presents arguments for their cause. Discuss the importance of planning the presentation, using persuasive arguments and selecting vocabulary for impact.

- Topic box. Provide a 'topic box' and cards for recording suitable debate topics. Each week select a topic, a chairperson and two small discussion groups. Have the remainder of the class take the role of audience and judges. At the conclusion of the activity, discuss the effectiveness of the arguments and the role of language in persuading or directing people's opinions.
- Reviews. Reviews are a more sophisticated form of report involving summary and value judgments. Before presenting reviews, discuss the importance of evaluating the content, forming opinions and using language to justify statements or persuade the listener. Initially, allow students to work in groups to prepare reviews on books, plays, films, TV programs etc.
- Panel discussions. Participate in panel discussions on current topics of interest or controversial issues, e.g. school uniforms, woodchipping, killing whales. Allocate time for panel members to read relevant material, clarify ideas and summarise information. During the discussion, the audience may note questions to ask or comments to make. These should be addressed after the presentation. At the conclusion of the activity, reflect on the speakers' effectiveness in summarising the main ideas of the topic, putting forward opinions or responding to other members of the panel.

Language and Thinking

(See p. 79)

At this stage, students are using language for independent, critical thinking. They deal with abstract ideas and express understandings using more refined and extended vocabulary. Teachers need to provide students with opportunities to use language to predict or formulate hypotheses, to clarify and express their thoughts and to interpret and evaluate information.

The *Oral Language: Resource Book* chapter *Language and Thinking* outlines strategies and activities for developing cognitive skills.

- Demonstrating knowledge. An effective method for demonstrating understanding of a topic is through telling someone else about it—peers, teachers or other adults. Informal sharing allows for more spontaneous interaction in which the listener can ask immediate questions to clarify information or clear up misunderstandings. More formal sharing requires careful thought and preparation. Provide a framework for planning.

- Problem solving. Students develop thinking skills when they use language to experiment, explore and solve problems. Take time to create open-ended tasks that can be approached in different ways and have a range of possible solutions. Focus on the language involved in thinking through the process rather than aiming to describe only the outcomes. Encourage students to explore together, experiment, observe, discuss and express their understandings to peers and adults:
  - work together to make a set of instructions without words, i.e. simply as drawings
  - invent a game from specified materials
  - make a 2-D representation from a 3-D model
  - complete manipulative puzzles, solve riddles and brain-teasers
  - investigate mathematics problems and brainstorm a range of solutions.

- Working in groups. Problems are easier to solve when students can share their thoughts and ideas with others. Organise partner or group activities where students must talk together to complete the task. When students interact they use language to refine their thinking skills, demonstrate and explain processes to others, or explore possibilities through discussion, questioning and observation:
  - discuss controversial issues in small groups, reach consensus on main points and present opinions to class
  - work with a partner to select and classify information
  - decide on most effective means of obtaining information before beginning a task, e.g. interview, survey, questionnaire
  - demonstrate and explain a process to others, e.g. cooking pancakes, making a cube from paper
  - write and perform a play together.

- Science. Before science investigations, give students time to predict, hypothesise and brainstorm possible outcomes. When students talk about what they see they clarify their observations and understandings. Talking also elicits questions, and consideration of these questions leads to further investigations:
  - encourage students to talk before investigations
  - work in groups to share ideas, predictions and explanations
  - work with a partner to list possible outcomes of investigations
  - include a sharing time at the end of investigations for verifying predictions, explaining solutions and evaluating group participation in the activity.

- Mathematics. Introduce mathematics activities that focus on partner or small-group organisation. Provide open-ended tasks that conclude with a sharing session to discuss solutions, strategies or new discoveries. Encourage students to refine and extend their vocabulary during discussion:
  - work with a partner to speculate on solutions, estimate answers and check results
  - work together to brainstorm and experiment with different methods of depicting information, e.g. diagram, drawing, graph
  - look for patterns in numbers, shapes, weights etc.
  - listen to a problem then restate it to a peer or adult.
- Classification. Assist students to develop thinking skills by classifying what they observe, know, read or discuss:
  - nominate criteria in science, social studies, mathematics activities
  - have students choose the criteria for classifying information, e.g. habits, physical features, durability
  - classify information using semantic grids.

- Before and after. Establish and draw upon students' knowledge when new topics are introduced:
  - discuss the topic and record information through brainstorming, semantic grids etc.
  - list questions that need to be answered
  - highlight areas of interest
  - plan activities related to the topic
  - review and evaluate completed activities.
- Questioning. Model how to ask questions to clarify information and gain information, or analyse and explore ideas. Use question words—*when, who, where, what*—that elicit different types of information. Introduce activities that motivate students to practise questioning skills:
  - have students work in groups to plan interview questions
  - introduce open-ended tasks that motivate students to speculate, question and explore a range of solutions
  - demonstrate how to ask open questions that allow for a range of interpretations and responses.
- Teacher's questions. Questions should be sufficiently challenging to raise the level of students' thinking and promote learning.

- Reading. Read a variety of literature and ask questions that motivate students to think about the text:
  - describe details—*what, when, who, how many*
  - recognise main idea
  - identify and describe supporting details
  - recognise cause and effect
  - identify character traits
  - make evaluative comments.
- Fun with language. Help students to extend the range of words understood and used:
  - select interesting words from stories, poems, songs and classify them according to length, letter patterns, meaning
  - create nonsense rhymes
  - mime words
  - talk about and draw idioms
  - tell 'tall stories', jokes and riddles.
- Listening. Encourage students to listen critically to interpret what is said by others.
- Distinguishing fact from fantasy. Listen to stories, poems, news reports etc. Identify elements of fact or fantasy and justify opinions.
- Distinguishing fact from opinion. Listen to peers' news reports or television broadcasts with the purpose of distinguishing fact from opinion. Collect and compare differing reports of the same event and discuss possible reasons for contradictions.
- Advertising techniques. Listen to a variety of television advertisements about a similar product, e.g. food, clothes, toys. Compare the advertisements and list the features aimed at persuading the buyer, e.g. music, graphics, tone of voice, age of actors, relevance of information provided.

- Using persuasion. Work in groups to produce television or radio commercials. Discuss the power of language to influence human behaviour.
- Debates. Organise class debates on controversial issues, e.g. pollution, smoking, road accidents. Discuss how verbal and non-verbal language can influence people's opinions.

For Parents

How can I help my child with speaking and listening?

- Encourage your child to develop a positive attitude towards speaking and listening so he/she will continue to develop confidence and a willingness to share ideas, feelings and experiences.
- Discuss school work, successes, concerns, interests and personal experiences.
- Respect your child's ideas, opinions and feelings. Encourage discussion which motivates your child to elaborate ideas, justify opinions, develop logical arguments and express feelings.
- Involve your child in adult conversations, when appropriate. These experiences will provide a range of language styles, ideas and vocabulary.
- Assist your child to express ideas in an orderly, fluent manner. For example, ask for an explanation of a game, a description of an item or a recount of an experience.
- Help your child to extend the range of words understood and used by introducing specialised vocabulary when talking about topics of mutual interest, e.g. current affairs or computer programs.
- Encourage your child to listen and respond courteously and appropriately to others, even when opinions expressed may differ from his or her own.
- Provide opportunities for your child to speak and listen for a variety of purposes, e.g. telling jokes and riddles for enjoyment, explaining or giving directions, describing and elaborating on details, predicting and justifying, or identifying cause and effect.
- Provide a good listening model by showing interest in, and responding to, your child's contributions. For example, discuss issues at mealtimes and encourage all family members to participate.
- Provide a wide range of reading materials and encourage your child to read and share ideas and opinions.
- Talk about school topics and assignments. Assist your child to locate and organise information from reference books, encyclopaedias etc. Talk about layout, contents, index, glossary etc.
- Assist your child to locate information in the community, e.g. the local library, city council, community service groups.
- Compare similarities and differences between a book your child has read and its movie version.
- Watch and discuss television news reports and current affairs programs. If a particular interest is shown in a subject or event, encourage your child to look for follow-up information in newspapers.
- Discuss the effects of language on the behaviour of others, e.g. the effects of advertising or the methods used to persuade people to watch or listen to certain television or radio programs.
- Buy puzzle books that include word games.
- Play commercial games that have a focus on word building and word knowledge.
- Talk about ways to remember how to spell difficult words, e.g. 'practice' the noun, has the noun 'ice' within it.
- Talk about the relationships between words, e.g. unicycle, bicycle and tricycle and linked by the word 'cycle'.
- Show your child how to use informational books found in your home, e.g. phone and street directories, encyclopaedias, dictionaries, atlases.
- Use your local library.

© Education Department of Western Australia. Published by Rigby Heinemann

PHASE 7 Proficient Language Use

In this phase speakers/listeners are able to monitor and control their use of language with confidence. They are aware of nuances of meaning and can manipulate their use of words effectively in response to perceived demands. They can use language to position themselves with audiences and are able to evaluate critically, social and cultural implications of texts.

Student 1:	*This father is one to rely and act on inspiration…*
Student 2:	*Yeah*
Student 1:	*… and someone who does things on the spur of the moment*
Student 2:	*I think his emotions get in the way of what he acts on.*
Student 1:	*Yeah, but if he hadn't've decided and his emotions hadn't worked like that, then Cedna wouldn't've found a husband.*
Student 2:	*I don't think so, Cedna was too proud.*
Student 1:	*Yes, I do agree, but he didn't.*
Student 2:	*Yes, but that has a bearing on her fate.*
Student 1:	*It does, but it's Cedna's life and Cedna can do what she likes.*
Student 2:	*She was forced … No she can't …*
Student 1:	*Cedna couldn't make the choice because she was too proud.*
Student 2:	*Well, it wasn't her fault.*
Student 1:	*She couldn't make the choice, other people were making it for her.*
Student 2:	*If she'd been more thoughful about what she was doing then her father wouldn't've come over and done that to her.*
Student 1:	*If she'd just anticipated what was going to happen …*
Student 2:	*With everything that you do, do you anticipate what happens in the future?*

This short transcript is part of a much larger discussion that demonstrates the following indicators:

◆ **uses language to include or exclude others, e.g. paraphrasing technical terms to include audience**
• in conflict situation acknowledges different points of view
• uses language effectively to support, share understandings and experiences with and to influence others
• paraphrases to clarify meaning
• uses paraphrasing and restating to confirm understanding as listener
• uses language effectively to negotiate issues
◆ **uses language critically to reflect and analyse spoken and written texts**
◆ **uses language to reflect on learning and to further develop understanding, for example, can access own reaction to particular ideologies and positions**
• uses language to construct effective arguments in relation to contentious issues
• is able to consider and reflect on two sides of an argument, make a judgement and find own position

Proficient Language Use Indicators

Language of Social Interaction
(See p. 95)

The speaker/listener:

◆ **uses language to include or exclude others, e.g. paraphrasing technical terms to include audience**
- responds sensitively in a range of different contexts to the demands of audience and purpose, e.g. when making a visitor from a different socio-cultural background welcome at a barbecue
- in conflict situation acknowledges different points of view
- uses language to help reduce conflict
- uses language effectively to support, share understandings and experiences with and to influence others
- recognises potential social 'conflict' and is able to use language effectively to defuse the situation, e.g. being aware of and tactfully retrieving a social blunder, diverting attention from a divisive area or highlighting common ground between potential adversaries
- paraphrases to clarify meaning
- uses paraphrasing and restating to confirm understanding as listener
- uses language effectively to negotiate issues.

Language and Literacy
(See p. 97)

The speaker/listener:

◆ **uses language critically to reflect on and analyse spoken and written texts**
◆ **uses text structures and language features confidently according to purpose, context and audience, in cooperation with peers**
◆ **uses strategies such as note-taking to summarise spoken texts or to prepare for an oral presentation**
- can compare and contrast different points of view
- is aware of the acceptable genre to suit context, audience and purpose and purposefully uses a deemed unacceptable genre to make an impact
- confidently and accurately uses subject-specific vocabulary
- uses quotations, similes and metaphors to enhance communication
- uses language effectively to achieve an effect, e.g. to conjure up a menacing atmosphere or to convey calmness and peace

- detects and challenges the use of words and phrases that impute stereotypes such as gender, age, race; and identifies language which conveys social values
- purposefully uses unbiased language.

Language and Thinking
(See p. 99)

The speaker/listener:

◆ **uses language to reflect on learning and to further develop understanding, for example, can access own reaction to particular ideologies and positions, or recognises when further information is required to clarify understandings**
- uses language to construct effective arguments in relation to contentious issues
- manipulates use of language through sarcasm, jokes and subtle humour
- recognises the power of the spoken word to influence human behaviour
- is able to consider and reflect on two sides of an argument, make a judgement and find own position.

Teaching Notes

In this phase, teaching is focused primarily on assisting students develop mature competencies in language use across all subject areas. The demands of context, purpose and audience are wide-ranging and often specialised. Teaching techniques do not differ in essence from those used for Phase Six, but they are transposed into much more sophisticated contexts. Demands and expectations are greater and the subtle uses of language to influence thinking are of paramount importance. The ability to stand back, reflect on and control language use is developing and extending.

Major Teaching Emphases

- Promote the use of subject-specific vocabulary
- Encourage students to work collaboratively as well as independently
- Present tasks which develop problem-solving skills
- Present tasks and texts which allow students to reflect on and critically assess linguistic structures and features
- Structure experiences which challenge students to analyse, select and use different styles of language to suit a range of audiences and purposes
- Provide texts which allow students to identify and evaluate the part non-verbal elements play in communicating, intentionally or unintentionally, a point of view
- Foster a critical awareness of the social and cultural functions of language
- Foster oral language as a tool which can function to challenge, persuade, entertain, negotiate, analyse, reflect and construct a particular hypothesis
- Provide access to texts of increasing complexity
- Provide access to texts which are outside students' personal experiences
- Provide texts and experiences which encourage students to identify and analyse how audiences can be positioned to interpret texts in particular ways

At all phases:
- ◆ **provide models of correct English**
- ◆ **ensure that students encounter a range of purposes, audiences and situations that challenge them to use language in many different ways**
- ◆ **allow time to practise the sounds, rhythms, words and structures of language**
- ◆ **make links between oral and written language**
- ◆ **encourage students to respond to a range of oral and visual treats**
- ◆ **value the processes of group interaction.**

◆ *All these entries are considered critical to the children's further development*

Language of Social Interaction

(See p. 93)

Point of View and Language Style

Students are asked to role play the reporting of a road accident to a police officer adopting the language of characters to bring out differences due to socio-cultural factors such as gender, race and class. Discuss issues of stereotyping.

The media can provide an excellent context for a discussion on points of view and language styles. An incident that receives world media coverage can be discussed. Different versions can be used as examples of using language to push and reinforce a specific point of view. It may be possible to compare the coverage of different television stations and newspapers. The use of emotive language and language that reinforces stereotypes can be highlighted.

It may be possible to extend this activity to examine the role of the media in everyday life and the way in which it shapes thinking and attitudes. Issues of the right to privacy versus the right of the public to have access to information can emerge. Instances of 'copycat' kidnapping or media exploitation of private emotion can be weighed against the need for public awareness of danger or the effect of anti-social behaviour on people's lives.

Mock Job Interviews

Stress research and preparation, courtesy, posture, appearance, fluency, the use of formal speech patterns and modes of address. It is often illuminating to ask students to role-play both interviewee and interviewer.

Oral Histories

Students can learn a great deal about the power and pitfalls of language use by collecting and presenting oral histories.

Interviewing skills are of paramount importance. Students will undertake a great deal of preparatory work, when they familiarise themselves with background information and formulate key questions which are aligned to events, times, perspectives and relationships. They will need to be aware, however, that they may need to change tack in mid-stream to draw out or capitalise on something that is said that may be unexpected, divergent and have the potential to be of great interest.

Oral historians find that the skill of the interviewer lies in creative and sensitive listening. If set questions are pursued regardless, many fascinating facets of the subject may be missed. The interviewer needs to analyse what is being said as it is being said, listening between and beyond the lines. Questions need to draw the subject out so that the

history moves beyond the set agenda and touches the human aspects of the experience. Students need to discover the power of the open-ended prompt and the stultifying effect of the closed question.

Students collecting oral histories should be encouraged to use tape recorders for two reasons. The first reason is that the nuances may be picked up that escaped notice at the time of the interview. The second is to enable the interviewer to reflect on her or his technique, focusing specially on interactions that were positive and productive and contrasting these with less successful moments.

Language of Negotiation and Planning

Before taking part in group activities, students can further develop planning skills and refine their use of negotiation as they take responsibility for the allocation of roles and responsibilities. Investigate ways of deflecting confrontation by dealing with conflict with good humour and flexibility. Help students to conclude such discussions by summarising the proceedings so that there is no room for misunderstanding or ambiguity.

Language of Collaboration

During group activities and discussion involve students in reflecting on group processes. Students can analyse why the group is working as it is and talk about the language used by various members of the group to facilitate interaction between participants. Group work can provide opportunities for furthering understandings about how to use the language of negotiation, invitation, recognition and affirmation. It is important that the focus is on the use of language rather than on personalities. It is sometimes illuminating to stop proceedings unexpectedly to carry out an analysis of group dynamics, looking at what is currently happening and at the ways in which language is being used. This should not happen too often or it becomes intrusive and disrupts the group processes.

Language of Instruction

Taking on the role of expert can lead to a consideration of many aspects of oral language use. Students can be encouraged to consider the background knowledge and experience of the 'learners', the purpose of the language, and the need to listen and respond to the audience. It can be helpful to video such sessions, if this is not too threatening to the 'expert'. Whether or not the session is recorded, a de-briefing and reflection time afterwards is essential. Students need to take part in self-assessment, asking themselves if they achieved their goals. Use of language could provide a major focus. Students could discuss the difference between what was said and what was meant; whether the 'learners' felt affirmed and encouraged or 'put down'; whether tentative suggestions were followed through and how reflective listening strategies such as paraphrasing and clarification were used successfully.

Give students opportunities to give oral directions to others, monitoring their own performance to ensure that directions are clear and comprehensive. Teach them to monitor audience response so that failure to comprehend is immediately detected and remediated.

Language of Power

Role play and drama can be used as a vehicle for exploring the use of language to reinforce power structures in society and in school. The use of language to include or exclude others can also be examined, e.g. the use of technical terms or 'in-house' language to ensure that a person is kept on the fringe of a social group. Demonstrate how intonation patterns can be used to create closure on an issue, and how, conversely, intonation patterns can be used to invite further communication.

Language of Conciliation

Help students to prepare for spoken encounters not only by carrying out research into the topic under focus, but also by considering the knowledge-base, needs and potential attitudes of participants. Role play mock incidents in which possible pitfalls have been identified and a range of strategies planned that might:

- circumvent the issue

- counter the issue by offering a range of possible solutions
- minimise the issue by presenting a wider or more generic scenario.

Non-Verbal Communication

It is important that students are aware of issues relating to non-verbal communication when talking with individuals or groups. Video recordings of debates, discussions and formal presentations can help students come to terms with many of the subtleties of non-verbal communication. Implications of intonation patterns can also be considered.

Language and Literacy
(*See p. 93*)

Multiple Readings/Interpretations of a Text

After completing the reading of a fictional text, novel or short story, students are invited to create a visual symbol which encapsulates the text. Students are required to explain and justify their symbols in relation to the text. Students then group similar symbols and discuss them. Any symbols that are at odds with the main group should also be noted. Links can then be made to dominant and resistant readings of texts.

Another activity that provides sensitive insights into the range of possible interpretations or readings of a text is to set up a situation whereby a text is read firstly from the points of view of the characters and then 'as' the designated character. A text is chosen that depicts a small number of characters interacting at a critical moment in their lives. Students, or groups of students, are initially asked to listen to the reading of the text from the point of view of one of the characters.

The reading is broken off half way through and each group comments on 'their' character, discussing reactions and feelings and hypothesising about possible outcomes. Students are then asked to 'become' the character and listen to the remainder of the text as that person. Most people find that this 'personification' of the character is different from simply listening from a specific point of view. At the end of the reading students are asked to imagine that the characters are meeting together five years later to talk about the past.

Discussion can become impassioned, partisan and highly emotional.

The final stage of the activity is undertaken as the participant groups reflect on the experience they have undertaken. Students discuss the process they have been through and their part in it and contribution to it. The original text is used as a reference. It will be found that, in almost all cases, students have 'read into' the text elements that are not actually there. This is particularly so if a student has identified with a character to the extent that her or his personal experience has mingled with that of the fictional person. This may occur, for instance, if the incident in the book is about estranged parents and their children.

Comments and conclusions should relate back to the phenomenon of 'multiple readings' of a text and move away from the specific activity, which should be seen to serve simply as a vehicle to aid understanding.

The activity can also be used to illustrate how an author 'positions' readers in relation to socio-cultural issues.

Using Literature to Learn to Detect Authorial Stance

Students can be encouraged to generalise their ability to detect the philosophical or political bias of a writer from written to oral texts. The use of language to generate a personal viewpoint in a novel can be compared with that of a speaker in a public forum. Help students to identify the assumptions upon which arguments and positions are built and encourage them to develop ways to challenge these assumptions, using examples from literature. Discuss logical inconsistencies and non-sequitors in written and oral texts.

Cross-curriculum use of language

Social Studies offers many opportunities to refine and extend students' use of language. Most political decisions have ethical implications, some of which are readily apparent and some of which only become apparent in hindsight. The way language is used to present the most favourable aspect of a decision or policy can be very illuminating. Science can also provide a fertile field for a study of language use. Increasingly it is being realised that many scientific research projects have major ethical implications and that these should be considered by concerned citizens rather than those who have a vested interest in promoting a project.

Public Speaking

Provide a wide range of opportunities for students to make oral presentations to large or small audiences, using a range of text forms. Help them to appear relaxed and at ease and to give the impression that a well prepared text is spontaneous and unrehearsed. Discuss style of presentation, the use of non-sexist or racist language and the need to respond to perceived audience reactions. Create situations where there is a need to depart from a prepared text in order to modify the context. Discuss time constraints and the need to abandon segments of a text in order to include the most crucial points if time runs out for one reason or another.

Language of Justification

Use activities such as 'Lifeboats' to enhance students' abilities to analyse, summarise and justify why certain characters or elements of a plot are essential to a narrative. Each member of a group is allocated a character or an incident and is required to justify its continuing existence in the book. If a student is unable to put forward convincing and logical arguments in favour of the retention of his or her person or event, it is thrown out of the lifeboat.

The Use of Literary Allusions and Other Devices

Encourage students to use appropriate quotations and references to support their arguments. Provide examples of an able-speaker's use of imagery and analogy. Show how the use of such devices may illuminate a point or may be used to deflect attention from an issue. Discuss the use of tone and style as devices that attract or distance audiences. Collect instances of the effective and ineffective use of humour to gain audience participation. Monitor the use of names in a hectoring manner or to create an illusion of intimacy. Talk about the way in which such devices can attract or repel the listener, e.g. the use of a given name by a car salesperson and by a skilled interviewer on the television. Discuss the ways in which people project their personalities through their use and manipulation of verbal and non-verbal communication.

Language and Thinking

(See p. 93)

Argument

Mock trials. These can be based on issues arising from texts and on historical or fictional issues and characters. Students role play judge, accused, lawyers for the defence and prosecution, witnesses and court officials. The jury is comprised by the remainder of the class. The jury base their assessment of the strongest argument, not on their own perceptions of case.

It may be possible to obtain original documents on which students can base their arguments. Students are often obliged to accept the textbook version of historical events as they seldom have access to raw data. It is important, however, that they are able to view events from the perspectives of participants as well as those of historians. Students may be able to research newspaper reports, contemporary accounts, letters, and government documents such as Royal Commission reports, pertaining to a specific episode in history. They will then realise that many different accounts were given of the same event and many different judgements were made by contemporary people, all of which were considered by them to be valid. They can also analyse the documents to examine the way in which language was used to influence audiences in the reporting of such incidents.

If students identify with a particular character and then prepare for a mock trial, they will find that their use of language is shaped by their context, their purpose and their audience. They will also find that their perspectives may change and may be different from those of other historians. Events and characters that could be treated in this way could be drawn from the English or North American civil wars, the Boer war, the battle of the Eureka Stockade or the siege at Glenrowan.

Satire

Acceptance speeches can be composed and delivered satirising the acceptance of an international award. Students can create satires of 'Oscar' acceptance speeches using exaggeration, repetition, puns and other satiric techniques.

Current programs or revues based on satire can be analysed and discussed. It may be interesting to view clips of old programs to see if they have retained a 'cutting edge' or if they have dated and are no longer relevant. Dated satire could be compared with satire that has stood the test of time, such as the writings of Oscar Wilde. Students could decide whether they think that the power of the satire is vested in the language or the topic, or both.

Propaganda

Students are asked to identify rhetorical techniques in two or three political speeches and then create their own speeches based on ridiculous promises such as, 'I will give you jam on Fridays'.

News items provide a rich context for a study of propaganda. Before current issues are investigated, it may be profitable to look at past conflicts and the ways in which they were represented to the public. The First World War, the Suez crisis, the Falklands war, the Vietnam war and the Cuban Missile incident will provide ample examples.

Students can then watch a current affairs program in order to detect hidden bias and propaganda. They can focus on what is said and what isn't; on basic premises that people are expected to accept without question and on the manner of presentation. They may find it interesting to re-present the news item from an opposing point of view. A further study could be undertaken of words that have become common usage as a result of recent propaganda, such as 'ethnic cleansing'.

The study could be extended into areas such as medicine, science and the environment. It may become apparent to students that sometimes propaganda is disguised as medical, legal or scientific 'knowledge' which audiences are expected to accept without question as the dictum of experts.

It is important that students are able to distinguish between matters of fact and opinion and the ways in which opinion may be subtly disguised as fact by persuasive speakers.

Tutorial Presentations

Presenting well-rehearsed arguments which are detailed and thought provoking to stimulate class discussion.

Think of Time 123

This activity is taken from page 126 of Tomorrow's Classroom Today by Brownlie, F., Close, S. and Windgren,L. Students form groups of three and take on the roles of participant, observer and casual agent. A focus question is given to each group. Each offers a point of view. After each point of view has been presented, shared understandings are constructed using the contributions of the whole group. Finally, critical attributes of the concept are identified.

Impromptu Problem Solving

As a surprise tactic, pose a problem and ask groups of students to solve it in a set time, e.g. ten minutes. The students must all agree and be able to identify each other's contributions. The solution can be presented in a dramatic, poetic or oral presentation. A period of reflection is held at the conclusion of the session when students think about their solution and discuss what contributed to their thinking, e.g. it may have been a television program, a conversation with a friend or a magazine article. Group processes are also discussed, for instance, the elements which helped to bring about a positive result or the interactions that led to negative responses.

Responding to Oral Presentations

Provide as many opportunities as possible for students to listen to external speakers, live, on radio or on television, in order to summarise and re-present their talks. Students should be able to note key ideas at the time of presentation so that the notes can afterwards be developed into logical and well-supported reconstructions of the talks.

PHASE 8 Advanced Language Use Indicators

In this phase, the adult speaker/listener shows sophisticated understanding of the power and effect of spoken language.
Meta-linguistic awareness is fully developed.

These indicators have been compiled in order to clarify the goals towards which adults are moving.

Language of Social Interaction

The speaker/listener:

◆ **shows sophisticated understanding of the power and effect of spoken language when speaking and listening**
- negotiates agreements in groups where there are disagreements or conflicting personalities, managing the discussions sensitively and intelligently and concluding them with positive summaries of achievement
- uses talk to explore complex concepts and ideas to clarify her/his own and others' understanding
- asserts sustained points of view or ideas to both familiar and unfamiliar audiences with determination and conviction but without aggression, condescension or disrespect
- critically examines own reactions to spoken texts; is alert to own vulnerability, to emotional and other seductive appeals and can dispassionately analyse the personal and linguistic reasons for this
- uses non-sexist and non-racist language
- anticipates likely disagreements between self and listeners, and structures material to minimise or overcome this by acknowledgement, for example: *'I feel you may disagree with me about this but would you mind waiting until I've finished before you put forward your point of view.'*

Language and Literacy

The speaker/listener:

◆ **interacts responsively, critically and confidently with both familiar and unfamiliar audiences on specialised topics in formal situations, and consistently achieves a variety of purposes in speech**
◆ **analyses the characteristics of intended audiences and demonstrates psychological and interpretative insights in choosing approaches**

that suit audiences; chooses language calculated to appeal emotionally to specific audiences
- identifies, challenges and justifies interpretations of the underlying assumptions, points of view and subtexts in spoken texts; identifies when what is said seems contrary to what the text itself suggests and justifies that interpretation with evidence from the text
- responds quickly and appropriately to people and situations to maintain an overall purpose; confidently and good-humouredly handles diversions and unexpected questions
- modifies content and approach when speaking to an unresponsive audience
- understands that people respond to both non-verbal and verbal elements of spoken language and works on enhancing interpersonal skills to improve communication with others.

Language and Thinking

The speaker/listener:

◆ **analyses spoken texts in terms of the socio-cultural values, attitudes and assumptions they convey**
◆ **responds to and analyses spoken texts outside own socio-cultural experience to enhance own knowledge and understanding**
◆ **identifies and analyses characteristics of a speaker's tone and style of presentation; what makes it bombastic, humorous, reasonable**
- examines texts for subtexts, significant inclusions or exclusions, for example, how males and females are presented, included or excluded
- discusses the power of language to reinforce or change values and attitudes
- infers meaning by using socio-cultural understanding of the purposes of particular text types and the motivations of individuals, such as public figures

- knows that vested interests may colour some individuals' views and listens carefully for clues to the subtext
- knows that the impartial appearance of text may be bogus and listens critically for bias, e.g. current affairs program items
- explores how analogies, imagery and other linguistic features affect the tone and mood of spoken texts and provide insight into the speaker's motives and opinions.

Part IV

Profiles of Oral Language Development

To make recording easier for teachers, student profile sheets, that can be photocopied, are included in this book. They enable teachers to record the progress of individual students, and to compile a class profile.

The following records are included
- student's profile sheets for self-assessment
- whole class profile sheets using all the indicators
- whole class profile sheets using key indicators only.

Note:
An individual student profile sheet that will record progress throughout the primary years is included as a fold-out at the beginning of this book.

Student's Profile Sheets

The student's profile sheets for each phase provide lists of skills, understandings, strategies and attitudes that both the student and teacher can look for when assessing oral language development.

Why use Student's Profile Sheets?

Students and teachers can work together to set and monitor goals in oral language development, using the profile sheets. Students could also be encouraged to show their parents when entries are made on the sheet.

How to use the Student's Profile Sheets

The profile sheets can be kept in student's personal files and updated from time to time, perhaps in student/teacher conferences. Young students may need help to use the sheets but older students can be encouraged to take responsibility for their own oral language development.

When would you use the Student's Profile Sheets?

The student's profile sheets can be used at regular intervals or incidentally during personal conferences.

PHASE 2: Early Language

Name: _____ Date: _____

Things I know and can do	not yet	some-times	always
• I know the names of lots of things.			
• I can play with words and sing to myself.			
• I can make people understand, even if I don't say things quite like they do.			
• I have my own special words for some things, like 'winscriper' for windscreen wiper.			
• I know what people mean when they say things like 'Put your mug on the table' or 'Put that box under the table' or 'Put your shoes behind the door'.			
• I am good at telling people about things, like where I have been or what I did on my walk, but I don't always talk like grown-ups.			
• I know that I should take turns when I'm talking with other people.			
• I know how to get people to listen to me when I say something.			
• I like talking to my toys and I often talk to myself.			
• I love listening to stories and joining in with the parts I know. I know when people leave bits out of stories and I can tell them what they should have said.			
• I love to look at books and can tell myself stories from books when I look at the pictures.			
• I love to say rhymes and sing songs with a grown-up.			
• I like to draw and 'write'.			
• I know the difference between things like big and little, fast and slow, wet and dry, now and 'in a minute', yesterday and tomorrow (or 'after one sleep'), heavy and light ('though I sometimes mix up heavy with big and light with small').			
• Sometimes I know why things happen, like why my shirt got torn or why the little table fell over.			
• Sometimes I can guess what might happen if…			
• I like to ask lots and lots of questions.			

PHASE 3: Exploratory Language

Name: _____ Date: _____

Things I know and can do	not yet	some-times	always
• I am good at telling people about things, like where I have been or what I have been doing and I love talking about what I've done.			
• I know how to talk to people nicely. I say things like 'please', 'thank you' and 'excuse me'.			
• I can join in when people are talking. I listen to them and tell them things they want to know.			
• Sometimes I like to talk like Mum or Dad, especially when I'm telling someone else what to do.			
• I ask questions when I don't understand something.			
• I try to explain what I mean if someone doesn't understand what I am saying.			
• I can tell people how I feel and why I feel the way I do.			
• I know lots of stories and songs and I can act them out if I want to.			
• I have fun playing make-believe games by myself and with my friends.			
• I can think of lots of different ways of doing things, like building a cubby house.			
• If I am asked what might happen next week, or next holidays or even next year, I am good at having a guess.			
• I ask lots and lots of questions about everything.			
• I know some 'book language' like 'Once upon a time...' and 'They lived happily ever after' and 'A long, long time ago...'			
• I can retell a story I know.			
• I can tell about how I feel and I often know how other people are feeling.			

PHASE 4: Emergent Language for Learning

Name: _____ Date: _____

Things I know and can do	not yet	some-times	always
• I can tell people what I hope and wish for and what I think about.			
• I know whether a sentence sounds right or not.			
• I'm getting better at listening and knowing what other people want.			
• I know what I want to say, and I say it, in class discussions.			
• I know that I talk in different ways to different people, like my friends, my teacher and important visitors.			
• When I am in the playground with my friends I talk in a different way from when I am in class.			
• I argue with people, but I don't always listen to what they are saying.			
• I retell a story so that people know where it happened, who it is about and what happened.			
• When I tell my news, I tell people what happened, where it happened and who was there.			
• I can say why something is different from or the same as something else, for instance, tennis, basketball, cricket and football are all played with balls, but the balls are all different.			
• I can usually work out why things happened, or guess what might happen in the future.			
• I love going around with my own special friends and I like to tell them 'secrets'.			

PHASE 5: Consolidated Language for Learning

Name: _____ Date: _____

Things I know and can do	not yet	some-times	always
• I know the right way to talk to people, and can easily change the way I speak when I am with different people, such as my friends, the Principal or visitors or in different places like a formal restaurant or a fast food eatery.			
• When I disagree with someone, I don't usually change my opinion at the time, but afterwards, when we talk it through with an adult, I can understand the other person's point of view.			
• I listen to what people say and am able to tell them how I feel about what is being said.			
• Sometimes when I am listening to adults I can 'read between the lines' and I know that they don't mean exactly what they say.			
• I know what I think about things, and I often talk things through with other people, telling them my opinion and listening to what they say.			
• If I am asked to tell people about something I have read or seen on the television, I can tell them about it accurately, describing important details and answering any questions they might have.			
• I can listen to someone speaking, for instance on the television, and make up my own mind about what they are saying.			
• I can read aloud with expression.			
• Before I start a written or spoken assignment I plan carefully so that my presentation is well thought out and interesting.			
• I like playing with language, using puns and jokes.			
• I know that the language used in fiction can be very different from the language of factual texts; and that the language of books is different from the language we use when we talk.			
• I am good at thinking of reasons why things have happened or may happen.			
• I like solving problems and can see that there might be several solutions to a problem.			
• I like working with other people as a member of a team.			

PHASE 6: Extended Language for Learning

Name: _____ Date: _____

Things I know and can do	not yet	some-times	always
• I can talk appropriately on formal and informal occasions.			
• When I have a disagreement with other people I am able to talk things through constructively. I realise that the other person has a valid point of view and we are usually able to reach some sort of agreement.			
• I listen and talk with other people when we are working together so that we solve problems collaboratively and achieve our goals.			
• When I give people directions, or explain something, I can tell whether or not they have understood what I am saying and adapt what I have said if need be.			
• If I am talking about something to a group of people, I am able to assess how much they already know and adjust what I am saying to meet their needs.			
• I am good at interpreting body language and facial expressions and am aware of the impact of my own body language on other people.			
• I can summarise events and episodes from life or from the news and give people accurate and comprehensive recounts of what occurred.			
• I plan content and structure carefully before making a presentation.			
• I enjoy discussing events, and topics we have been studying.			
• I like taking part in sessions when we think critically about issues, discussing our own prejudices and that of others and the ways in which people are stereotyped in our society.			
• I can argue effectively, considering and weighing up all points of view and making reasonable judgements on the basis of the evidence which is put forward.			
• I often make predictions and hypotheses and can collect and present evidence in support of my position.			
• I answer questions clearly and succinctly.			

Whole Class Profile Sheets

The class profile sheets have all indicators from the Oral Language Developmental Continuum presented phase by phase so that teachers can enter information about children's progress in oral language. The sheets can be photocopied as required.

Why use Class Profile Sheets?

The class profile sheets enable teachers to develop a comprehensive class profile on which to base planning and programming decisions.

How to use the Class Profile Sheets?

- Observe children's talking and listening behaviours
- Highlight indicators observed
- Write entry date and highlighter colour used

When would you use Class Profile Sheets?

Although teachers make ongoing observations of children's progress, they may formally update information on the continuum two or three times each year (perhaps before report times).

CLASS

PHASE 1: BEGINNING LANGUAGE INDICATORS

Students' Names

The Child:

- develops a repertoire of cries to satisfy biological needs
- cries, chuckles, gurgles, coos
- 'babbles' and repeats sound patterns
- constantly plays at making sounds, alone or with others
- recognises human voices
- responds to own name
- uses voice to attract attention
- uses sound to signify emotions, e.g. anger, excitement
- voices many sounds which resemble those of first language, e.g. ma-ma, da-da
- uses non-verbal gestures, e.g. waves
- produces first real words
- co-ordinates gestures and words, e.g. waves and says *Bye*
- uses single words and two-word phrases to convey meaning: *drink* - I want a drink *go way* - Go away
- uses non-verbal communication to support single and two-word utterances: *drink* - points to fridge
- understands more language than can be verbalised
- may overgeneralise word meanings to represent many ideas: *bed* may mean bed, pillow, blanket, going to bed
- has favourite words, e.g. *No! Mine!*
- relates messages which are supported by facial expression or intonation: *Mummy car! Mummy car?*

continued on next page

Teacher's Notes:

Dates:

CLASS ───────────

PHASE 1: BEGINNING LANGUAGE INDICATORS (continued)

Students' Names

The Child:

- may make mispronunciations:
  tu   for cup
  free   for tree
  ress   for dress
  rink   for drink

- mixes words, e.g.
  shakemilk   milkshake

- has control over some functional language, e.g. *in, on, out, down*

- may produce parents' speech sounds without meaning, e.g. in attempting to hold a conversation with a visitor

- understands simple questions

- follows simple directions

- begins to question for information

- engages in language games, e.g. *Round and round the garden, Incy wincy spider*

Teacher's Notes:

Dates:

CLASS _____

PHASE 2: EARLY LANGUAGE INDICATORS

Students' Names

The Child:

Speech Development

◆ uses own grammar style which is an approximation of adult grammar—overgeneralisations are common, e.g.

plurals	sheeps for sheep
verbs	goed for went
auxiliary verbs	I did run fast

- experiments with sounds through rhyme and repetition

- is beginning to use pronouns but may make errors in syntax, e.g. *Look at the doggie. They is big.*

- shows confusion between pairs of terms, e.g. *I/you, this/that, here/there*

- demonstrates an understanding of distinction in personal pronouns, e.g. *Give it to him. Give it to me.*

- begins to use endings such as *ing, ed, s*

- may confuse tenses when describing an event, e.g. *I going shopping yesterday*

- uses function words—*is, was, a, the, for, because*—to link ideas previously expressed in unconnected ways: *Me go park*—becomes *I'm going to the park*

- demonstrates an understanding of most common prepositions, e.g. *on, under, front, behind*

- may make sound substitutions, e.g.

b for v	*dribe* for drive
t for k	*tick* for kick
s for sh	*sip* for ship
w for r	*wabbit* for rabbit
d for th	*brudda* for brother
f for th	*free* for three

- focuses on interesting sounding words and enjoys repeating them, e.g. *beautiful* - bb-oo-di-fool

Language of Social Interaction

◆ is beginning to develop awareness of listener needs and begins to provide feedback information when introducing new topic, e.g. Nanna, I went shopping. Look at this.

- is aware of social conventions but does not match actions to phrases, e.g. 'scuse me' and pushes friend with the blocks.

continued on next page

Teacher's Notes:

Dates:

CLASS _____

PHASE 2: EARLY LANGUAGE INDICATORS (continued)

Student's Names

The Child:

Language of Social Interaction (continued)

- co-ordinates gesture and tone of voice to convey meaning, e.g. *I love you, Mum* (cuddles)
- refines conversation skills, e.g. learns ways to enter conversation, takes turns during an interaction
- talks aloud to self
- engages in imaginary play, often using toys or other props
- converses with imaginary friends

Language and Literacy

- ◆ gives simple descriptions of past events
- shows an interest in listening to and talking about stories
- asks for and joins in stories
- 'reads' books aloud, often assigning own meaning to print
- tells 'stories' about pictures in books
- begins to develop an understanding of story structure, e.g. notices when a page is not read from a favourite book
- 'pretend reads' to other children, dolls, toys
- retells simple stories
- demonstrates an awareness of rhyme
- reads familiar print in the environment
- acts out stories or repeats phrases encountered in books
- draws symbols and 'reads' the message
- shows an interest in the meaning of words encountered in books.

continued on next page

Teacher's Notes:

Dates:

CLASS _____

PHASE 2: EARLY LANGUAGE INDICATORS (continued)

Students' Names

The Child:

Language and Thinking

◆ **shows an interest in explanations of how and why**

• is able to express an opinion, e.g. 'I don't like...'

• is beginning to develop concepts of quantity, size, speed, time

• begins to see relations between objects, e.g. puts toys together, building blocks

• is beginning to understand cause and effect, e.g. *My tower fell over 'cos I put this big block on top*

• begins to verbalise reasons

• makes simple predictions of future events, e.g. *We'll be going in two more sleeps*

• offers solutions and explanations to a situation, e.g. *It sank 'cos it was full*

• expresses feelings

• constantly questions - *why, who, what, where, when*

• may demonstrate confusion between fantasy and reality, e.g. *I didn't break it. Monster did.*

Teacher's Notes:

Dates:

© Education Department of Western Australia. Published by Rigby Heinemann

CLASS _____

PHASE 3: EXPLORATORY LANGUAGE

The Child:

Speech Development

◆ **has grasped most grammatical rules but may still overgeneralise, e.g.**
tenses   swimmed for swam, kept for kept
plurals   mouses for mice
pronouns they put the book in there

• may still produce non-fluent speech

• may make minor mispronunciations, e.g. *s/w* for th, *fw* for sw

• uses more lengthy and complex sentences, tending to overuse *and, then*

Language of Social Interaction

◆ **contributes appropriately to classroom interactions, showing or expressing**
puzzlement if something is not understood

◆ **adapts language for social control, requests and for seeking information**

• is aware of the impact of language in conflict situations. Often uses adults to deal with conflict

• sustains one-to-one conversation with children and adults

• takes conversational turns as speaker and listener

• is beginning to use polite conversational conventions, e.g. *Excuse me*

• can only see one course of action when in conflict, e.g. *I **want that pen***

Language and Literacy

◆ **includes when, who, where, what in recounts**

• uses language to describe objects, events and feelings

• is beginning to develop a vocabulary for language concepts, e.g. 'sound', 'word', 'sentence'

• engages in imaginative play, using language to negotiate roles, scenes and maintenance of play

• distinguishes between, and describes, past and present experiences

• relates stories from a sequence of 2-4 pictures.

continued on next page

Teacher's Notes:

Dates:

Students' Names

Whole Class Profile Sheet

CLASS _____

PHASE 3: EXPLORATORY LANGUAGE (continued)

Student's Names

The Child:

Language and Literacy (continued)

- uses story language, e.g. *Once upon a time...*
- may combine fantasy and reality when describing or retelling
- initiates and joins in playground chants and rhymes

Language and Thinking

- ◆ **uses language to explain, enquire and compare**
- makes inferences, e.g. *I can't play outside if it's raining*
- describes words in terms of function, e.g. *You ride a horse, You drive a car*
- may display confusion when using pairs of comparative terms, e.g. *more/less, big/little*
- projects into the future, anticipates and predicts, e.g. *If you blow that balloon up any more, it'll burst* or *When we go on holiday we'll need...*
- discusses events, concepts of objects not experienced
- suggests possible alternatives when problem-solving, e.g. *If we use that cardboard box instead of the wood, we'd be able to bend it*
- shows an understanding of cause and effect
- constantly questions
- reflects on own and others' feelings, e.g. *I got mad at Nathan when he took my toys* or *It makes you sad, does it, Mum?*

Teacher's Notes:

Dates:

CLASS _____

PHASE 4: EMERGENT LANGUAGE FOR LEARNING

Students' Names

The Speaker/Listener:

Speech Development

◆ **judges whether a sentence is grammatically correct and adapts accordingly**

- has grasped most grammatical rules but may still overgeneralise, e.g.
  - verbs   *sleeped* for slept
  - plurals *mouses* for mice

- is beginning to use some complex grammatical connectives to sustain a topic, e.g. *because, if, after*

- uses cognitive verbs, e.g. *think, like, want,* etc. to express thoughts, wishes, dreams

- uses slang and jargon with peers

Language of Social Interaction

◆ **uses tone, volume, pace, intonation pattern and gesture to enhance meaning**

◆ **takes into account audience and purpose when speaking**

◆ **can sustain a conversation with a variety of audiences, e.g. teacher, peers, parents**

- takes conversational turns as speaker and listener

- responds to classroom expectations of polite behaviour, e.g. *Could you pass me..., I'm sorry.* Waits for turn before speaking

- participates in group discussions

- distinguishes between language used in different situations, e.g. 'home language', 'classroom language' and 'playground language'.

continued on next page

Teacher's Notes:

Dates:

Whole Class Profile Sheet

CLASS

PHASE 4: EMERGENT LANGUAGE FOR LEARNING (continued)

Student's' Names

The Speaker/Listener:

Language and Literacy

◆ develops specific vocabulary to suit different purposes, e.g. language for description, classification, comparison, argument

◆ shows evidence of language cohesion;
  (a) narrative logical, sequenced retells
  (b) recounts sequenced by time order
  (c) conversation sustained, on topic

• includes *when, who, where, what* in recounts

• shows a knowledge of story structure by describing, comparing or contrasting, setting, characters, events, conclusion, etc. in narrative texts

• uses language to express grammatical forms encountered in narrative texts, e.g. *Once upon a time... ...and they lived happily ever after*

• engages in more elaborate role play of characters or events encountered in stories

Language and Thinking

◆ uses language to predict and recall

◆ uses language to interact with peers, e.g. collaborative activities

• demonstrates abstract thinking by using verbs of cognition to express thoughts, hypotheses, wishes, e.g. *I wonder, hope, understand, think, believe, wish*

• uses language to describe similarities and differences

• uses language to categorise objects, people, places, events, etc.

• uses language to discuss cause and effect

• uses language to reason and argue.

continued on next page

Teacher's Notes:

Dates:

CLASS _____

PHASE 4: EMERGENT LANGUAGE FOR LEARNING (continued)

Student's' Names

The Speaker/Listener:

Language and Thinking (continued)

- is beginning to distinguish between language forms and language meanings, e.g. *Pull your socks up* means *Improve your behaviour*
- is beginning to understand humour in jokes and riddles
- follows instructions, e.g. classroom routines, relaying messages
- plans and gives instructions in a variety of situations, formal and informal, e.g. classroom routines, peer teaching
- questions to clarify or gain further information
- explains cause and effect, e.g. *She fell off the bar because she was trying a somersault for the first time, then her hand slipped*
- follows instructions that include two or three elements.

Teacher's Notes:

Dates:

Whole Class Profile Sheet

© Education Department of Western Australia. Published by Rigby Heinemann

CLASS

Students' Names

PHASE 5: CONSOLIDATED LANGUAGE FOR LEARNING

The Speaker/Listener:

Language of Social Interaction

◆ communicates effectively by sharing ideas, offering advice, opinion and information and reacting to the contributions of others

• shows an increasing awareness of social conventions, e.g. *Could you tell me where...? Mrs Carroll asked if you would...*

• reacts according to own perceptions in a conflict situation, but is able to appreciate another's point of view through adult mediation

• adapts language to meet different social and situational needs, talking to friends at netball is different from meeting friends of parents

• monitors others' speech and paraphrases content, e.g. *I felt really angry when the group wouldn't co-operate*

• uses intonation, facial expressions and gestures as tools for communicating ideas and feelings

• uses jargon or slang with peers

Language and Literacy

◆ recognises that language is adapted to meet different social, situational and educational needs, e.g. the language of reporting is different from the language of interviewing or story-telling

◆ demonstrates the ability to develop a topic in curriculum-related situations, e.g. reporting, describing, comparing

◆ interprets texts from own point of view—expresses opinions, draws conclusions

◆ uses appropriately specialised vocabulary and structures in a variety of situations, e.g. discussions, reports, modified debates

• shows evidence of planning during recounts

• adds appropriate elaboration and detail to recounts and describes events, objects and concepts outside immediate experience, e.g. community news

• adds evaluative comments to enhance spoken presentations, e.g. *I believe that recycling is very important and we all need to take it a lot more seriously*

• demonstrates knowledge of difference between narrative and informational texts.

continued over the page

Teacher's Notes:

Dates:

Students' Names										

CLASS

PHASE 5: CONSOLIDATED LANGUAGE FOR LEARNING (continued)

The Speaker/Listener:

Language and Literacy (continued)

- incorporates literary expressions when describing or discussing narrative texts, e.g. repetition of the phrase made the story flow

- is able to succinctly describe the setting, events and characters of stories/films/television dramas

- retells stories of some complexity, individually or in groups

- makes comparisons between narrative and informational texts

- uses similes and metaphors to enhance meaning

- shows knowledge of language structure, e.g. uses conjunctions effectively to express relationships between ideas; maintains and manipulates tones and mood appropriately; provides referents when using pronouns

- discusses rules of language, grammar

- recognises subtle differences in words, e.g. shimmery/shiny, cross/angry, eat/devour

- is able to describe the significant content of stories, television dramas and films succinctly.

continued over the page

Teacher's Notes:

Dates:

CLASS

PHASE 5: CONSOLIDATED LANGUAGE FOR LEARNING (continued)

Student's Names

The Speaker/Listener:

Language and Thinking

◆ **continues to develop reason and logic, by attempting to draw conclusions, make inferences, justify and explain statements; asking questions and seeking confirmation**

◆ **listens to evaluate, draw inferences and make judgements**

• investigates problems and sees a range of solutions,

• offers definitions of words, usually by functions

• considers possible cause/effect relationships and justifies the most appropriate, e.g. *At first I thought it was the slope that increased the car speed but it could also be the smooth surface of the track*

• follows complex sequences of instructions

• evaluates the consistency of information across several sentences

• initiates questions to gain clarification or further information

• uses language for puns, jokes, riddles and sarcasm.

Teacher's Notes:

Dates:

CLASS _____

PHASE 6: EXTENDED LANGUAGE FOR LEARNING

The Speaker/Listener:

Language of Social Interaction

◆ **selects and sustains language and style appropriate to purpose, context and audience, e.g. formal, informal talk**

◆ **effectively interprets whether a message has been understood**

• takes into account another's point of view, e.g. _from your point of view this might be expensive but the benefits for the animals are of vital importance._

• needs and uses language to moderate or reduce the conflict

• uses appropriate social conventions

• is aware of audience and purpose, e.g. 'This presentation is on the history of mining in this area. As you already know about early exploration, I will not go into too much detail about events prior to 1880'

• refines use of appropriate facial expressions and gestures to communicate ideas, feelings and information.

Language and Literacy

◆ **summarises main ideas from written or spoken texts using succinct language**

◆ **draws conclusions from, makes inferences based on and evaluates written and oral text and is able to listen and respond to an alternative perspective**

◆ **describes events, objects and concepts outside immediate experience, e.g. world news**

• shows advanced planning of content when presenting information, e.g. in reports, summaries

• selects vocabulary for impact, e.g. to persuade, surprise

• uses language to reflect on and discuss written or spoken texts

• confidently and competently recounts events, providing detail and elaboration

• demonstrates fluency and a personal style when reading orally

• discusses rules of language, grammar.

continued over the page

Teacher's Notes:

Dates:

CLASS

Students' Names

PHASE 6: EXTENDED LANGUAGE FOR LEARNING (continued)

The Speaker/Listener:

Language and Thinking

◆ **uses language to express independent, critical thinking**

◆ **uses oral language to formulate hypotheses, criticise, evaluate, plan and to influence the thinking of others**

◆ **deals with abstract ideas using concrete examples**

• listens to the ideas and viewpoints of others, using oral language to respond, expressing and modifying own opinions

• presents a variety of arguments to support a claim

• compares and contrasts observations, ideas, hypotheses with others

• explains understandings of topics, concepts, etc. providing convincing argument and evidence to support point of view

• recognises potential and limitations of words to persuade, explain, clarify, solve problems etc.

• answers spontaneous questions in an informed, competent manner, making sure that listeners understand what is being said

• uses language to paint 'word pictures'.

Teacher's Notes:

Dates:

CLASS _____

Student's Names

PHASE 7: PROFICIENT LANGUAGE USE

The Speaker/Listener:

Language of Social Interaction

◆ **uses language to include or exclude others, e.g. paraphrasing technical terms to include audience**

• responds sensitively in a range of different contexts to the demands of audience and purpose, e.g. when making a visitor from a different socio-cultural background welcome at a barbecue

• in conflict situation acknowledges different points of view

• uses language to help reduce conflict

• uses language effectively to support, share understandings and experiences with and to influence others

• recognises potential social 'conflict' and is able to use language effectively to defuse the situation, e.g. being aware of and tactfully retrieving a social blunder, diverting attention from a divisive area or highlighting common ground between potential adversaries

• paraphrases to clarify meaning

• uses paraphrasing and restating to confirm understanding as listener

• uses language effectively to negotiate issues.

Language and Literacy

◆ **uses language critically to reflect on and analyse spoken and written texts**

◆ **uses text structures and language features confidently according to purpose, context and audience, in cooperation with peers**

◆ **uses strategies such as note-taking to summarise spoken texts or to prepare for an oral presentation**

• can compare and contrast different points of view

• is aware of the acceptable genre to suit context, audience and purpose and purposefully uses a deemed unacceptable genre to make an impact

• confidently and accurately uses subject-specific vocabulary

• uses quotations, similes and metaphors to enhance communication.

continued over the page

Teacher's Notes:

Dates:

CLASS _____

Students' Names

PHASE 7: PROFICIENT LANGUAGE USE (continued)

The Speaker/Listener:

Language and Literacy (continued)

- uses language effectively to achieve an effect, e.g. to conjure up a menacing atmosphere or to convey calmness and peace

- detects and challenges the use of words and phrases that impute stereotypes such as gender, age, race; and identifies language which conveys social values

- purposefully use unbiased language

Language and Thinking

- ◆ uses language to reflect on learning and to further develop understanding, for example, can access own reaction to particular ideologies and positions, or recognises when further information is required to clarify understandings

- uses language to construct effective arguments in relation to contentious issues

- manipulates use of language through sarcasm, jokes and subtle humour

- recognises the power of the spoken word to influence human behaviour

- is able to consider and reflect on two sides of an argument, make a judgement and find own position.

Teacher's Notes:

Dates:

© Education Department of Western Australia. Published by Rigby Heinemann

CLASS _____

PHASE 8: ADVANCED LANGUAGE USE

Student's Names

The Speaker/Listener:

Language of Social Interaction

◆ **shows sophisticated understanding of the power and effect of spoken language when speaking and listening**

• negotiates agreements in groups where there are disagreements or conflicting personalities, managing the discussions sensitively and intelligently and concluding them with positive summaries of achievement

• uses talk to explore complex concepts and ideas to clarify her/his own and others' understanding

• asserts sustained points of view or ideas to both familiar and unfamiliar audiences with determination and conviction but without aggression, condescension or disrespect

• critically examines own reactions to spoken texts; is alert to own vulnerability, to emotional and other seductive appeals and can dispassionately analyse the personal and linguistic reasons for this

• uses non-sexist and non-racist language

• anticipates likely disagreements between self and listeners, and structures material to minimise or overcome this by acknowledgement, for example: _'I feel you may disagree with me about this but would you mind waiting until I've finished before you put forward your point of view'._

Language and Literacy

◆ **interacts responsively, critically and confidently with both familiar and unfamiliar audiences on specialised topics in formal situations, and consistently achieves a variety of purposes in speech**

◆ **analyses the characteristics of intended audiences and demonstrates psychological and interpretative insights in choosing approaches that suit audiences; chooses language calculated to appeal emotionally to specific audiences**

• identifies, challenges and justifies interpretations of the underlying assumptions, points of view and subtexts in spoken texts; identifies when what is said seems contrary to what the text itself suggests and justifies that interpretation with evidence from the text

• responds quickly and appropriately to people and situations to maintain an overall purpose; confidently and good-humouredly handles diversions and unexpected questions.

continued over the page

Teacher's Notes:

Dates:

Whole Class Profile Sheet

CLASS

PHASE 8: ADVANCED LANGUAGE USE (continued)

© Education Department of Western Australia. Published by Rigby Heinemann

Student's' Names

The Speaker/Listener:

Language and Literacy (continued)

- modifies content and approach when speaking to an unresponsive audience

- understands that people respond to both non-verbal and verbal elements of spoken language and works on enhancing interpersonal skills to improve communication with others

Language and Thinking

◆ analyses spoken texts in terms of the socio-cultural values, attitudes and assumptions they convey

◆ responds to and analyses spoken texts outside own socio-cultural experience to enhance own knowledge and understanding

◆ identifies and analyses characteristics of a speaker's tone and style of presentation; what makes it bombastic, humorous, reasonable

- examines texts for subtexts, significant inclusions or exclusions, for example, how males and females are presented, included or excluded

- discusses the power of language to reinforce or change values and attitudes

- infers meaning by using socio-cultural understanding of the purposes of particular text types and the motivations of individuals, such as public figures

- knows that vested interests may colour some individuals' views and listens carefully for clues to the subtext

- knows that the impartial appearance of text may be bogus and listens critically for bias, e.g. current affairs program items

- explores how analogies, imagery and other linguistic features affect the tone and mood of spoken texts and provide insight into the speaker's motives and opinions.

Teacher's Notes:

Dates:

Whole Class Profile Sheets
Key Indicators Only

Why use the Key Indicator Profile Sheets?

The Key Indicators can be used by teachers to quickly ascertain children's stages of oral language development and obtain an accurate class profile. The information can be used by teachers to plan future teaching and allocate resources appropriately.

How to use the Key Indicator Profile Sheets?

- Observe children's speaking and listening behaviours
- Highlight indicators observed
- Write entry date and highlighter colour used

When would you use Key Indicator Profile Sheets?

Teachers may use these sheets to get a quick profile of a new class or to help when reporting to parents. Schools may decide on set times (say twice each year) for this information to be collected and analysed.

© Education Department of Western Australia. Published by Rigby Heinemann

Students' Names

KEY INDICATORS

PHASE 2: Early Language

The Child:

Speech Development

◆ uses own grammar style which is an approximation of adult grammar —
overgeneralisations are common, e.g.
plurals   sheeps for sheep
verbs   goed for went
auxiliary verbs   I did run fast

Language of Social Interaction

◆ is beginning to develop awareness of listener needs and begins to provide
feedback information when introducing new topic, e.g. Nanna, I went shopping.
Look at this.

Language and Literacy

◆ gives simple descriptions of past events

Language and Thinking

◆ shows an interest in explanations of how and why

PHASE 3: Exploratory Language

The Child:

Speech Development

◆ has grasped most grammatical rules but may still overgeneralise, e.g.
tenses   swimmed for swam, keept for kept
plurals   mouses for mice
pronouns   they put the book in there

Language of Social Interaction

◆ contributes appropriately to classroom interactions, showing or expressing
puzzlement if something is not understood

◆ adapts language for social control, requests and for seeking information

Language and Literacy

◆ includes when, who, where, what in recounts.

continued on next page

Teacher's Notes:

Dates:

KEY INDICATORS (continued)

PHASE 3: Exploratory Language (continued)

The Child:

Language and Thinking

◆ uses language to explain, enquire and compare.

PHASE 4: Emergent Language for Learning

The Speaker/Listener:

Speech Development

◆ judges whether a sentence is grammatically correct and adapts accordingly

Language of Social Interaction

◆ uses tone, volume, pace, intonation pattern and gesture to enhance meaning

◆ takes into account audience and purpose when speaking

◆ can sustain a conversation with a variety of audiences, e.g. teacher, peers, parents

Language and Literacy

◆ develops specific vocabulary to suit different purposes, e.g. language for description, classification, comparison, argument

◆ shows evidence of language cohesion;
  (a) narrative logical, sequenced retells
  (b) recounts sequenced by time order
  (c) conversation sustained, on topic

Language and Thinking

◆ uses language to predict and recall

◆ uses language to interact with peers, e.g. collaborative activities.

continued over the page

Teacher's Notes:

Dates:

Students' Names

CLASS

KEY INDICATORS (continued)

Students' Names

PHASE 5: Consolidated Language for Learning

The Speaker/Listener:

Language of Social Interaction

◆ communicates effectively by sharing ideas, offering advice, opinion and information and reacting to the contributions of others

Language and Literacy

◆ recognises that language is adapted to meet different social, situational and educational needs, e.g. the language of reporting is different from the language of interviewing or story-telling

◆ demonstrates the ability to develop a topic in curriculum-related situations, e.g. reporting, describing, comparing

◆ interprets texts from own point of view—expresses opinions, draws conclusions

◆ uses appropriately specialised vocabulary and structures in a variety of situations, e.g. discussions, reports, modified debates

◆ continues to develop reason and logic, by attempting to draw conclusions, make inferences, justify and explain statements; asking questions and seeking confirmation

◆ listens to evaluate, draw inferences and make judgements.

PHASE 6: Extended Language for Learning

The Speaker/Listener:

Language of Social Interaction

◆ selects and sustains language and style appropriate to purpose, context and audience, e.g. formal, informal talk

◆ effectively interprets whether a message has been understood

Language and Literacy

◆ summarises main ideas from written or spoken texts using succinct language

◆ draws conclusions from, makes inferences based on and evaluates written and oral text and is able to listen and respond to an alternative perspective

◆ describes events, objects and concepts outside immediate experience, e.g. world news.

continued over the page

Teacher's Notes:

Dates:

KEY INDICATORS (continued)

Student's Names

Language and Thinking

◆ uses language to express independent, critical thinking

◆ uses oral language to formulate hypotheses, criticise, evaluate, plan and to influence the thinking of others

◆ deals with abstract ideas using concrete examples.

PHASE 7: Proficient Language Use

The Speaker/Listener:

Language of Social Interaction

◆ uses language to include or exclude others, e.g. paraphrasing technical terms to include audience

Language and Literacy

◆ uses language critically to reflect on and analyse spoken and written texts

◆ uses text structures and language features confidently according to purpose, context and audience, in cooperation with peers

◆ uses strategies such as note-taking to summarise spoken texts or to prepare for an oral presentation

Language and Thinking

◆ Uses language to reflect on learning and to further develop understanding, for example, can access own reaction to particular ideologies and positions, or recognises when further information is required to clarify understandings.

continued over the page

Teacher's Notes:

Dates:

Student's' Names

KEY INDICATORS (continued)

PHASE 8: Advanced Language Use

The Speaker/Listener:

Language of Social Interaction

◆ shows sophisticated understanding of the power and effect of spoken language when speaking and listening

Language and Literacy

◆ interacts responsively, critically and confidently with both familiar and unfamiliar audiences on specialised topics in formal situations, and consistently achieves a variety of purposes in speech

◆ analyses the characteristics of intended audiences and demonstrates psychological and interpretative insights in choosing approaches that suit audiences; chooses language calculated to appeal emotionally to specific audiences

Language and Thinking

◆ analyses spoken texts in terms of the socio-cultural values, attitudes and assumptions they convey

◆ responds to and analyses spoken texts outside own socio-cultural experience to enhance own knowledge and understanding

◆ identifies and analyses characteristics of a speaker's tone and style of presentation; what makes it bombastic, humorous, reasonable

Teacher's Notes:

Dates:

Acknowledgements

The Development Continua were written by the FIRST STEPS TEAM under the direction of Alison Dewsbury.

The First Steps project acknowledges the invaluable contributions made by the schools and teachers listed below and by all the school principals who have supported their staffs as they participated in the First Steps Project: **Challis** and **Grovelands Early Childhood Education Centres, Tuart Hill Junior Primary School** and **Glen Forrest Primary School** were involved in action research that focused on the use of different Continua.

The Project received a great deal of assistance from the following Primary Schools: **Carey Park, Hollywood, Medina, Midvale, Mingenew, West Busselton, Wilson, Kalgoorlie Central, Boulder,** and **Boulder Junior Primary School.**

The Project is also grateful to **Wagin District High School** in the Narrogin District and the schools in the Esperance District—the **Bremer Bay, Castletown, Condingup, Esperance, Fitzgerald, Gairdner, Grass Patch, Jerdacuttup, Lake King, Munglinup, Nulsen, Ongerup** and **Varley Primary Schools**, which, with **Jerramungup** and **Ravensthorpe District High Schools**, achieved so much in an associate role between 1989 and 1991. These schools provided examples of exemplary practice and documentation that enabled the Project team to refine and extend aspects of First Steps.

The Gosnells Oral Language Project was initiated by **Wirrabirra Education Support Unit** and Ashburton Drive, **Gosnells, Huntingdale, Seaforth** and **Wirrabirra Primary Schools** under the leadership of **Leanne Allen** and **Judith Smailes**. First Steps supported this project with funding, editorial and publishing assistance.

First Steps and Aboriginal Children

Warakurna, Wingellina and **Blackstone Schools** took part in the **Ngaanyatjarra Lands Project** coordinated by Sandi Percival. Action research was carried out in these schools, evaluating the use of the First Steps Developmental Continua and related materials with children from the Central Desert. Funding was provided by the ESL unit.

Fitzroy Crossing District High School, Gogo and **Wangkajungka Primary Schools** participated in a special project designed to adapt the Continua and strategies to the needs of children in Kimberley schools. **Margi Webb** and **Chris Street** worked with colleagues to accomplish this task. In 1991 and 1992 the following schools continued to address the literacy learning of Aboriginal students as part of a special project: in the **Narrogin District, Narrogin Primary School** and **Pingelly** and **Wagin District High Schools**; in the Kalgoorlie District, **Menzies Primary School** and **Laverton** and **Leonora District High Schools** in the Karratha District,

Roebourne and **Onslow Primary Schools**; in the Kimberley District, **Dawul** and **Jungdranung Primary Schools** and **Kununurra District High School**; and in the Bayswater District, **Midvale Primary School**.

First Steps and Children For Whom English is a Second Language

The Highgate Primary School, with its **Intensive Language Centre**, has undertaken a special project designed to ensure that First Steps meets the needs of children for whom English is a second or foreign language. **Anna Sinclair** was the coordinator of this Project. Extensive work, coordinated by **Kay Kovalevs**, has also been carried out at **Christmas Island District High School**.

The following schools were involved in the initial trials of the First Steps, Student Database computer program: **Belmay, Boulder, Bremer Bay, Carey Park, Carnarvon, Condingup, East Hamilton Hill, East Maddington, Jerramungup, Koondoola, Leonora, Medina, Midvale, Montrose, Nulsen, Orelia, Queens Park, Ravensthorpe, Tranby, Whiteside** and **Wilson Primary Schools, Wagin District High School** and **Boulder Junior Primary School**. These schools trialled the program during the last half of fourth term 1990. It is because of them that the Database was able to be developed satisfactorily.

A special mention must be made of the **First Steps Collaborative Teachers** who have given so much to the Project. Their expertise, hard work, dedication and unfailing cheerfulness have been commented on by all who have worked with them. They typify excellence in teaching practice and professionalism.

Finally, special thanks must go to the children who have contributed their writing.

Bibliography

Brown, H. & Cambourne, B. 1987, *Read and Retell*, Thomas Nelson, Melbourne

Cambourne, B. 1988, *The Whole Story*, Ashton Scholastic, Auckland, NZ

Cutting, B. 1990, *Talk Your Way to Reading*, Shortland Publications Limited, NZ

Davidson, A. 1983, *Maths and Me (Helping Your Child with Mathematics)*, Rigby Education, Sydney

Dwyer, J. (ed.), *A Sea of Talk*, Primary English Teaching Association, Rozelle, NSW

Education Department of South Australia, Publications Branch (1981), *Listening and Speaking: R–7 Language Arts*

Education Department of South Australia, Publications Branch (1989), *Learning in Early Childhood. What Does it Mean in Practice?*

Education Department of Western Australia, Curriculum Branch (1981), *Oral Language in the Classroom*, Government Printer, Perth

Education Department of Western Australia, Curriculum Branch (1982), *Small Group Work in the Classroom*, Government Printer, Perth

Education Department of Western Australia, Curriculum Branch (1983), *Reading K–7 Teachers Notes*, Government Printer, Perth

Education Department of Western Australia, Curriculum Branch (1986) *Writing K–7 Teachers Notes*, Government Printer, Perth

Education Department of Western Australia, Curriculum Branch (n.d.), *Speaking and Listening K–7 Teachers Notes, (Draft Ed.)*, Government Printer, Perth

Furniss, E. & Green, P. 1991, *The Literacy Agenda*, Eleanor Curtain Publishing, Melbourne

Johnson, T. D. & Louise, D. R. 1985, *Literacy Through Literature*, Methuen Australia, Melbourne

Liddelow, L. 1983, *Talk With Me — Language Development Through Poems, Stories and Plays*, Longman Cheshire Pty Limited, Melbourne

Mallan, K. 1991, *Children as Storytellers*, Primary English Association, Newtown, NSW

McCracken, M. & R. 1989, *Whole Language Themes — Animals— Ideas for Teachers*, Longman Cheshire Pty Limited, Melbourne

Parkes, B. 1990, *Stories to Tell Teacher's Book*, Oxford University Press, Melbourne

Tough, J. 1977, *Talking and Learning: A Guide for Fostering Communication Skills in Nursery and Infant Schools*, Ward Lock Educational for The Schools Council, London, UK